Let's Keep in Touch

Follow Us   Online

Visit US at

Online Math Lessons

It's easy! Here's how it works.

1- Request a FREE introductory session.

2- Meet a Math tutor online.

3- Start Learning Math in Minutes.

Send Email to: info@EffortlessMath.com

www.EffortlessMath.com

… So Much More Online!

- FREE Math lessons

- More Math learning books!

- Online Math Tutors

Looking for an Online Math Tutor?

Send Email to: info@EffortlessMath.com

PSAT Mathematics Workbook 2018 - 2019

A Comprehensive Review and Step-By-Step Guide to Preparing for the PSAT Math

By

Reza Nazari & Ava Ross

Copyright © 2018

Reza Nazari & Ava Ross

All inquiries should be addressed to:

info@effortlessMath.com

www.EffortlessMath.com

ISBN-13: 978-1721734849

ISBN-10: 1721734848

Published by: Effortless Math Education

www.EffortlessMath.com

Description

PSAT Mathematics Workbook is full of specific and detailed material that will be key to succeeding on the PSAT Mathematics. It's filled with the critical math concepts a student will need in order to do well on the test. Math concepts in this book break down the topics, so the material can be quickly grasped. Examples are worked step–by–step, so you learn exactly what to do.

This comprehensive PSAT Mathematics workbook brings together everything a student needs to know for the Mathematics section of the PSAT test. It is designed to address the needs of PSAT test takers who must have a working knowledge of basic Math. It contains most common sample questions that are most likely to appear in the Mathematics section of the PSAT. This book leaves no stones unturned!

PSAT Mathematics Workbook with over 2,500 sample questions and 2 complete PSAT Mathematics tests is all a student needs to fully prepare for the PSAT Math test. It will help the student learns everything they need to ace the math section of the test.

This workbook includes practice test questions. It contains easy–to–read essential summaries that highlight the key areas of the PSAT Mathematics test. Effortless Math test study guide reviews the most important components of the PSAT Math test. Anyone planning to take the PSAT test should take advantage of the review material and practice test questions contained in this study guide.

Inside the pages of this comprehensive book, students can learn basic math operations in a structured manner with a complete study program to help them understand essential math skills. It also has many exciting features, including:

- Dynamic design and easy–to–follow activities
- Step–by–step guide for all Math topics
- Targeted, skill–building practices
- A fun, interactive and concrete learning process

- Math topics are grouped by category, so you can focus on the topics you struggle on
- All solutions for the exercises are included, so you will always find the answers
- 2 Complete PSAT Math Practice Tests that reflect the format and question types on PSAT

PSAT Mathematics Workbook is the ideal prep solution for any student who wants to prepare for the PSAT test. It efficiently and effectively reinforces learning outcomes through engaging questions and repeated practice, helping students to quickly master basic Math skills.

Effortless Math books have helped thousands of students prepare for standardized tests and achieve their education and career goals. This is done by setting high standards and preparing the best quality Mathematics learning books, and this book is no exception. It is the perfect study aid for the PSAT Mathematics test. The student will definitely be well prepared for the test with this comprehensive workbook!

About the Author

Reza Nazari is the author of more than 100 Math learning books including:

– **Math and Critical Thinking Challenges:** For the Middle and High School Student
– **ACT Math in 30 Days**
– **ASVAB Math Workbook 2018 – 2019**
– **Effortless Math Education Workbooks**
– **and many more Mathematics books ...**

Reza is also an experienced Math instructor and a test–prep expert who has been tutoring students since 2008. Reza is the founder of Effortless Math Education, a tutoring company that has helped many students raise their standardized test scores—and attend the colleges of their dreams. Reza provides an individualized custom learning plan and the personalized attention that makes a difference in how students view math.

To ask questions about Math, you can contact Reza via email at:
reza@EffortlessMath.com

Find Reza's professional profile at:
goo.gl/zoC9rJ

Contents

CHAPTER 1: Fractions and Decimals 11

Simplifying Fractions... 13

Adding and Subtracting Fractions... 14

Multiplying and Dividing Fractions... 15

Adding Mixed Numbers.. 16

Subtract Mixed Numbers.. 17

Multiplying Mixed Numbers... 18

Dividing Mixed Numbers.. 19

Comparing Decimals... 20

Rounding Decimals 21

Adding and Subtracting Decimals... 22

Multiplying and Dividing Decimals... 23

Converting Between Fractions, Decimals and Mixed Numbers 24

Factoring Numbers... 25

Greatest Common Factor.. 26

Least Common Multiple.. 27

Answers of Worksheets – CHAPTER 1 28

Chapter 2: Real Numbers and Integers...33

Adding and Subtracting Integers 34

Multiplying and Dividing Integers... 35

Ordering Integers and Numbers 36

Arrange, Order, and Comparing Integers 37

Order of Operations.. 38

Mixed Integer Computations 39

Integers and Absolute Value... 40

Answers of Worksheets – CHAPTER 2 41

Chapter 3: Proportions and Ratios..44

Writing Ratios 45

Simplifying Ratios.. 46

Create a Proportion 47

Similar Figures... 48

Simple Interest 49

Ratio and Rates Word Problems 50

Answers of Worksheets – Chapter 3 51

Chapter 4: Percent 53

Percentage Calculations 54

Converting Between Percent, Fractions, and Decimals 55

Percent Problems 56

Markup, Discount, and Tax 57

Answers of Worksheets – Chapter 4 58

Chapter 5: Algebraic Expressions 60

Expressions and Variables 61

Simplifying Variable Expressions 62

Simplifying Polynomial Expressions 63

Translate Phrases into an Algebraic Statement 64

The Distributive Property 65

Evaluating One Variable 66

Evaluating Two Variables 67

Combining like Terms 68

Answers of Worksheets – Chapter 5 69

Chapter 6: Equations 71

One–Step Equations 72

Two–Step Equations 73

Multi–Step Equations 74

Answers of Worksheets – Chapter 6 75

Chapter 7: Inequalities 76

Graphing Single–Variable Inequalities 77

One–Step Inequalities 78

Two–Step Inequalities 79

Multi–Step Inequalities 80

Answers of Worksheets – Chapter 7 81

Chapter 8: Linear Functions 83

Finding Slope 84

Graphing Lines Using Slope–Intercept Form 85

Graphing Lines Using Standard Form...86

Writing Linear Equations...87

Graphing Linear Inequalities 88

Finding Midpoint...89

Finding Distance of Two Points 90

Answers of Worksheets – Chapter 8 91

Chapter 9: Polynomials 95

Classifying Polynomials 96

Writing Polynomials in Standard Form 97

Simplifying Polynomials 98

Adding and Subtracting Polynomials 99

Multiplying Monomials 100

Multiplying and Dividing Monomials 101

Multiplying a Polynomial and a Monomial 102

Multiplying Binomials 103

Factoring Trinomials 104

Operations with Polynomials...105

Answers of Worksheets – Chapter 9..106

Chapter 10: Quadratic and System of Equations...110

Solve a Quadratic Equation...111

Solving Systems of Equations by Substitution 112

Solving Systems of Equations by Elimination..113

Systems of Equations Word Problems 114

Answers of Worksheets – Chapter 10...115

Chapter 11: Quadratic Functions 116

Graphing quadratic functions in standard form 117

Graphing quadratic functions in vertex form 118

Solving quadratic equations by factoring 119

Use the quadratic formula and the discriminant..120

Operations with complex numbers 121

Solve quadratic inequalities..122

Answers of Worksheets – Chapter 11 123

Chapter 12: complex numbers 128

Adding and subtracting complex numbers 129

Multiplying and dividing complex numbers 130

Graphing complex numbers 131

Rationalizing imaginary denominators 132

Answers of Worksheets – Chapter 12 133

Chapter 13: Exponents and Radicals 135

Multiplication Property of Exponents 136

Division Property of Exponents 137

Powers of Products and Quotients 138

Zero and Negative Exponents 139

Negative Exponents and Negative Bases 140

Writing Scientific Notation 141

Square Roots 142

Answers of Worksheets – Chapter 13 143

Chapter 14: Statistics 146

Mean, Median, Mode, and Range of the Given Data 147

Box and Whisker Plots 148

Bar Graph 149

Stem–And–Leaf Plot 150

The Pie Graph or Circle Graph 151

Scatter Plots 152

Answers of Worksheets – Chapter 14 153

Chapter 15: Geometry 156

The Pythagorean Theorem 157

Area of Triangles 158

Perimeter of Polygons 159

Area and Circumference of Circles 160

Area of Squares, Rectangles, and Parallelograms 161

Area of Trapezoids 162

Answers of Worksheets – Chapter 15 163

Chapter 16: Solid Figures 164

　Volume of Cubes 165

　Volume of Rectangle Prisms 166

　Surface Area of Cubes 167

　Surface Area of a Rectangle Prism 168

　Volume of a Cylinder 169

　Surface Area of a Cylinder 170

　Answers of Worksheets – Chapter 16 171

Chapter 17: Logarithms 172

　Rewriting logarithms 173

　Evaluating logarithms 174

　Properties of logarithms 175

　Natural logarithms 176

　Solving exponential equations requiring logarithms 177

　Solving logarithmic equations 178

　Answers of Worksheets – Chapter 17 179

Chapter 18: Matrices 181

　Adding and subtracting matrices 182

　Matrix multiplication 183

　Finding determinants of a matrix 184

　Finding inverse of a matrix 185

　Matrix equations 186

　Answers of Worksheets – Chapter 18 188

Chapter 19: Functions Operations 191

　Function notation 192

　Adding and subtracting functions 193

　Multiplying and dividing functions 194

　Composition of functions 195

　Answers of Worksheets – Chapter 19 196

Chapter 20: Probability 197

　Probability of Simple Events 198

　Factorials 199

Permutations 200

Combination... 201

Answers of Worksheets – Chapter 20.. 202

Chapter 21: Trigonometric Functions 204

Trig ratios of general angles.. 205

Sketch each angle in standard position 206

Finding coterminal angles and reference angles 207

Writing each measure in radians 208

Writing each measure in degrees 209

Evaluating each trigonometric function 210

Missing sides and angles of a right triangle 211

Arc length and sector area 212

Answers of Worksheets – Chapter 21.. 214

PSAT Mathematics Practice Tests 218

PSAT Mathematics Practice Tests Answers and Explanations.......................... 271

CHAPTER 1: Fractions and Decimals

Math Topics that you'll learn today:

- ✓ Simplifying Fractions
- ✓ Adding and Subtracting Fractions
- ✓ Multiplying and Dividing Fractions
- ✓ Adding Mixed Numbers
- ✓ Subtract Mixed Numbers
- ✓ Multiplying Mixed Numbers
- ✓ Dividing Mixed Numbers
- ✓ Comparing Decimals
- ✓ Rounding Decimals
- ✓ Adding and Subtracting Decimals
- ✓ Multiplying and Dividing Decimals
- ✓ Converting Between Fractions, Decimals and Mixed Numbers
- ✓ Factoring Numbers
- ✓ Greatest Common Factor
- ✓ Least Common Multiple
- ✓ Divisibility Rules

"A Man is like a fraction whose numerator is what he is and whose denominator is what he thinks of himself. The larger the denominator, the smaller the fraction." –Tolstoy

Simplifying Fractions

Helpful Hints		Example:
	– Evenly divide both the top and bottom of the fraction by 2, 3, 5, 7, … etc. – Continue until you can't go any further.	$\dfrac{4}{12} = \dfrac{2}{6} = \dfrac{1}{3}$

✎ *Simplify the fractions.*

1) $\dfrac{22}{36} = \dfrac{11}{18}$

2) $\dfrac{8}{10} = \dfrac{4}{5}$

3) $\dfrac{12}{18} = \dfrac{6}{9} = \dfrac{2}{3}$

4) $\dfrac{6}{8} = \dfrac{3}{4}$

5) $\dfrac{13}{39} = \dfrac{1}{3}$

6) $\dfrac{5}{20} = \dfrac{1}{4}$

7) $\dfrac{16}{36} = \dfrac{8}{18} = \dfrac{4}{9}$

8) $\dfrac{18}{36} = \dfrac{1}{2} =$

9) $\dfrac{20}{50} = \dfrac{2}{5}$

10) $\dfrac{6}{54} = \dfrac{1}{9}$

11) $\dfrac{45}{81} = \dfrac{5}{9}$

12) $\dfrac{21}{28} = \dfrac{3}{4}$

13) $\dfrac{35}{56} = \dfrac{5}{8}$

14) $\dfrac{52}{64} = \dfrac{26}{32} = \dfrac{13}{16}$

15) $\dfrac{13}{65} = \dfrac{1}{5}$

16) $\dfrac{44}{77} = \dfrac{4}{7}$

17) $\dfrac{21}{42} = \dfrac{1}{2}$

18) $\dfrac{15}{36} = \dfrac{5}{12}$

19) $\dfrac{9}{24} = \dfrac{3}{8}$

20) $\dfrac{20}{80} = \dfrac{1}{4}$

21) $\dfrac{25}{45} = \dfrac{5}{9}$

Adding and Subtracting Fractions

Helpful

Hints

– For "like" fractions (fractions with the same denominator), add or subtract the numerators and write the answer over the common denominator.
– Find equivalent fractions with the same denominator before you can add or subtract fractions with different denominators.
– Adding and Subtracting with the same denominator:

$$\frac{a}{b} + \frac{c}{b} = \frac{a+c}{b}$$
$$\frac{a}{b} - \frac{c}{b} = \frac{a-c}{b}$$

– Adding and Subtracting fractions with different denominators:

$$\frac{a}{b} + \frac{c}{d} = \frac{ad+cb}{bd}$$
$$\frac{a}{b} - \frac{c}{d} = \frac{ad-cb}{bd}$$

✎ **Add fractions.**

1) $\frac{2}{3} + \frac{1}{2} = \frac{7}{6} = 1\frac{1}{6}$

2) $\frac{3}{5} + \frac{1}{3} = \frac{14}{15}$

3) $\frac{5}{6} + \frac{1}{2} = 1\frac{1}{3}$

4) $\frac{7}{4} + \frac{5}{9} = \frac{83}{36} = 2\frac{11}{36}$

5) $\frac{2}{5} + \frac{1}{5} = \frac{3}{5}$

6) $\frac{3}{7} + \frac{1}{2} = \frac{13}{14}$

7) $\frac{3}{4} + \frac{2}{5} = \frac{23}{20} = 1\frac{3}{20}$

8) $\frac{2}{3} + \frac{1}{5} = \frac{13}{15}$

9) $\frac{16}{25} + \frac{3}{5} = \frac{31}{25} = 1\frac{6}{25}$

✎ **Subtract fractions.**

10) $\frac{4}{5} - \frac{2}{5} = \frac{2}{5}$

11) $\frac{3}{5} - \frac{2}{7} = \frac{11}{35}$

12) $\frac{1}{2} - \frac{1}{3} = \frac{1}{6}$

13) $\frac{8}{9} - \frac{3}{5} = \frac{13}{45} = 1\frac{1}{45}$

14) $\frac{3}{7} - \frac{3}{14} = \frac{3}{14}$

15) $\frac{4}{15} - \frac{1}{10} = \frac{5}{30}$

16) $\frac{3}{4} - \frac{13}{18} = \frac{7}{36}$

17) $\frac{5}{8} - \frac{2}{5} = \frac{9}{40}$

18) $\frac{1}{2} - \frac{1}{9} = \frac{7}{18}$

Multiplying and Dividing Fractions

Helpful *Hints*	– **Multiplying fractions:** multiply the top numbers and multiply the bottom numbers. – **Dividing fractions:** Keep, Change, Flip Keep first fraction, change division sign to multiplication, and flip the numerator and denominator of the second fraction. Then, solve!	**Example:** $$\frac{a}{b} \times \frac{c}{d} = \frac{a \times c}{b \times d}$$ $$\frac{a}{b} \div \frac{c}{d} = \frac{a}{b} \times \frac{d}{c} = \frac{ad}{bc}$$

✍ **Multiplying fractions. Then simplify.**

1) $\frac{1}{5} \times \frac{2}{3} = \frac{2}{15} = \frac{1}{5}$

2) $\frac{3}{4} \times \frac{2}{3} = \frac{1}{2} = \frac{1}{2}$

3) $\frac{2}{5} \times \frac{3}{7} = \frac{6}{35}$

4) $\frac{3}{8} \times \frac{1}{3} = \frac{1}{8} =$

5) $\frac{3}{5} \times \frac{2}{5} = \frac{6}{25}$

6) $\frac{7}{9} \times \frac{1}{3} = \frac{7}{27}$

7) $\frac{2}{3} \times \frac{3}{8} = \frac{1}{4}$

8) $\frac{1}{4} \times \frac{1}{3} = \frac{1}{12}$

9) $\frac{5}{7} \times \frac{7}{12} = \frac{5}{12}$

✍ **Dividing fractions.**

10) $\frac{2}{9} \div \frac{1}{4} = \frac{8}{9}$

11) $\frac{1}{2} \div \frac{1}{3} = \frac{3}{2} = 1\frac{1}{2}$

12) $\frac{6}{11} \div \frac{3}{4} = \frac{8}{11} =$

13) $\frac{11}{14} \div \frac{1}{10} = \frac{110}{14} = 7\frac{6}{7}$

14) $\frac{3}{5} \div \frac{5}{9} = \frac{27}{25} = 1\frac{2}{25}$

15) $\frac{1}{2} \div \frac{1}{2} = 1$

16) $\frac{3}{5} \div \frac{1}{5} = 3$

17) $\frac{12}{21} \div \frac{3}{7} = \frac{12}{9} = 1\frac{1}{3}$

18) $\frac{5}{14} \div \frac{9}{10} = \frac{50}{126} = \frac{25}{63}$

Adding Mixed Numbers

Helpful	Use the following steps for both adding and subtracting mixed numbers.	**Example:**
Hints	– Find the Least Common Denominator (LCD) – Find the equivalent fractions for each mixed number. – Add fractions after finding common denominator. – Write your answer in lowest terms.	$1\frac{3}{4} + 2\frac{3}{8} = 4\frac{1}{8}$

✎**Add.**

1) $4\frac{1}{2} + 5\frac{1}{2} = 10$

2) $2\frac{3}{8} + 3\frac{1}{8} = 5\frac{1}{2}$

3) $5\frac{3}{5} + 5\frac{1}{5} = 10\frac{4}{5}$

4) $1\frac{1}{3} + 2\frac{2}{3} = 4$

5) $5\frac{1}{6} + 5\frac{1}{2} = 10\frac{2}{3}$

6) $3\frac{1}{3} + 1\frac{1}{3} = 4\frac{2}{3}$

7) $1\frac{10}{11} + 1\frac{1}{3} = 3\frac{8}{33}$

8) $2\frac{3}{6} + 1\frac{1}{2} = 4$

9) $5\frac{3}{5} + 5\frac{1}{5} = 10\frac{4}{5}$

10) $7 + \frac{1}{5} = 7\frac{1}{5}$

11) $1\frac{5}{7} + \frac{1}{3} = 2\frac{1}{21}$

12) $2\frac{1}{4} + 1\frac{2}{4} = 3\frac{3}{4}$

16

Subtract Mixed Numbers

Helpful	Use the following steps for both adding and subtracting mixed numbers.	**Example:**
Hints	Find the Least Common Denominator (LCD) – Find the equivalent fractions for each mixed number. – Add or subtract fractions after finding common denominator. – Write your answer in lowest terms.	$5\frac{2}{3} - 3\frac{2}{7} = 2\frac{8}{21}$

✎ *Subtract.*

1) $4\frac{1}{2} - 3\frac{1}{2} = 1$

2) $3\frac{3}{8} - 3\frac{1}{8} = \frac{1}{4}$

3) $6\frac{3}{5} - 5\frac{1}{5} = 1\frac{2}{5}$

4) $2\frac{1}{3} - 1\frac{2}{3} = \frac{2}{3}$

5) $6\frac{1}{6} - 5\frac{1}{2} = \frac{2}{3}$

6) $3\frac{1}{3} - 1\frac{1}{3} = 2$

7) $2\frac{10}{11} - 1\frac{1}{3} = 1\frac{19}{33}$

8) $2\frac{1}{2} - 1\frac{1}{2} = 1$

9) $6\frac{3}{5} - 2\frac{1}{5} = 4\frac{2}{5}$

10) $7\frac{2}{5} - 1\frac{1}{5} = 6\frac{1}{5}$

11) $2\frac{5}{7} - 1\frac{1}{3} = 1\frac{8}{21}$

12) $2\frac{1}{4} - 1\frac{1}{2} = \frac{3}{4}$

Multiplying Mixed Numbers

Helpful	1- Convert the mixed numbers to improper fractions.	Example:
	2- Multiply fractions and simplify if necessary.	$2\frac{1}{3} \times 5\frac{3}{7} =$
Hints	$a\frac{c}{b} = a + \frac{c}{b} = \frac{ab+c}{b}$	$\frac{7}{3} \times \frac{38}{7} = \frac{38}{3} = 12\frac{2}{3}$

✎ *Find each product.*

1) $1\frac{2}{3} \times 1\frac{1}{4}$

$\frac{5}{3} \times \frac{5}{4} = \frac{25}{12} = 2\frac{1}{12}$

2) $1\frac{3}{5} \times 1\frac{2}{3}$

$\frac{8}{5} \times \frac{5}{3} = \frac{8}{3} = 2\frac{2}{3}$

3) $1\frac{2}{3} \times 3\frac{2}{7}$

$\frac{5}{3} \times \frac{23}{7} = \frac{115}{21} = 5\frac{10}{21}$

4) $4\frac{1}{8} \times 1\frac{2}{5}$

$\frac{33}{8} \times \frac{7}{5} = \frac{231}{40} = 5\frac{31}{40}$

5) $2\frac{2}{5} \times 3\frac{1}{5}$

$\frac{12}{5} \times \frac{16}{5} = \frac{192}{25} = 7\frac{17}{25}$

6) $1\frac{1}{3} \times 1\frac{2}{3}$

$\frac{4}{3} \times \frac{5}{3} = \frac{20}{9} = 2\frac{2}{9}$

7) $1\frac{5}{8} \times 2\frac{1}{2}$

$\frac{13}{8} \times \frac{5}{2} = \frac{65}{16} = 4\frac{1}{16}$

8) $3\frac{2}{5} \times 2\frac{1}{5}$

$\frac{17}{5} \times \frac{11}{5} = \frac{187}{25} = 7\frac{12}{25}$

9) $2\frac{2}{3} \times 4\frac{1}{4}$

$\frac{8}{3} \times \frac{17}{4} = \frac{34}{3} = 11\frac{1}{3}$

10) $2\frac{3}{5} \times 1\frac{2}{4}$

$\frac{13}{5} \times \frac{6}{4} = \frac{78}{20} = 3\frac{9}{10}$

11) $1\frac{1}{3} \times 1\frac{1}{4}$

$\frac{4}{3} \times \frac{5}{4} = \frac{5}{3} = 1\frac{2}{3}$

12) $3\frac{2}{5} \times 1\frac{1}{5}$

$\frac{17}{5} \times \frac{6}{5} = \frac{102}{25} = 4\frac{2}{25}$

Dividing Mixed Numbers

Helpful *Hints*	1- Convert the mixed numbers to improper fractions. 2- Divide fractions and simplify if necessary. $$a\frac{c}{b} = a + \frac{c}{b} = \frac{ab+c}{b}$$

Example:

$$2\frac{1}{3} \times 5\frac{3}{7} =$$

$$\frac{7}{3} \times \frac{38}{7} = \frac{38}{3} = 12\frac{2}{3}$$

✎**Find each quotient.**

1) $2\frac{1}{5} \div 2\frac{1}{2}$

$\frac{11}{5} \times \frac{2}{5} = \frac{22}{25}$

2) $2\frac{3}{5} \div 1\frac{1}{3}$

$\frac{13}{5} \times \frac{3}{4} = \frac{39}{20} = 1\frac{19}{20}$

3) $3\frac{1}{6} \div 4\frac{2}{3}$

$\frac{19}{6} \times \frac{3}{14} = \frac{19}{28}$

4) $1\frac{2}{3} \div 3\frac{1}{3}$

$\frac{5}{3} \times \frac{3}{10} = \frac{1}{2}$

5) $4\frac{1}{8} \div 2\frac{2}{4}$

$\frac{33}{8} \times \frac{4}{10} = \frac{33}{20} = 1\frac{13}{20}$

6) $3\frac{1}{2} \div 2\frac{3}{5}$

$\frac{7}{2} \times \frac{5}{13} = \frac{35}{26} = 1\frac{9}{26}$

7) $3\frac{5}{9} \div 1\frac{2}{5}$

$\frac{32}{9} \times \frac{5}{7} = \frac{160}{63} = 2\frac{34}{63}$

8) $2\frac{2}{7} \div 1\frac{1}{2}$

$\frac{16}{7} \times \frac{2}{3} = \frac{32}{21} = 1\frac{11}{21}$

9) $3\frac{1}{5} \div 1\frac{1}{2}$

$\frac{16}{5} \times \frac{2}{3} = \frac{32}{15} = 2\frac{2}{15}$

10) $4\frac{3}{5} \div 2\frac{1}{3}$

$\frac{23}{5} \times \frac{3}{7} = \frac{69}{35} = 1\frac{34}{35}$

11) $6\frac{1}{6} \div 1\frac{2}{3}$

$\frac{37}{6} \times \frac{3}{5} = \frac{111}{30} = 3\frac{21}{30}$

12) $2\frac{2}{3} \div 1\frac{1}{3}$

$\frac{8}{3} \times \frac{3}{4} = 2$

Comparing Decimals

Helpful	-	**Decimals:** is a fraction written in a special form. For example, instead of writing $\frac{1}{2}$ you can write 0.5.	**Example:**
Hints	-	**For comparing:** Equal to = Less than < greater than > greater than or equal ≥ Less than or equal ≤	2.67 > 0.267

✏️ *Write the correct comparison symbol (>, < or =).*

1) 1.25 < 2.3

2) 0.5 > 0.23

3) 3.2 = 3.2

4) 4.58 < 45.8

5) 2.75 > 0.275

6) 5.2 > 5

7) 3.1 > 0.31

8) 6.33 > 0.733

9) 8 > 0.8

10) 4.56 > 0.456

11) 1.12 < 1.14

12) 2.77 < 2.78

13) 6.08 < 6.11

14) 1.11 > 0.211

15) 2.6 > 2.55

16) 1.24 < 1.25

17) 5.52 > 0.552

18) 0.33 > 0.033

19) 14.4 = 14.4

20) 0.05 < 0.50

21) 0.59 < 0.7

22) 0.5 > 0.05

23) 0.90 = 0.9

24) 0.27 < 0.4

Rounding Decimals

Helpful	We can round decimals to a certain accuracy or number of decimal places. This is used to make calculation easier to do and results easier to understand, when exact values are not too important.	**Example:**
Hints	First, you'll need to remember your place values:	$\underline{6}.37 = 6$

12.4567

1: tens	2: ones	4: tenths
5: hundredths	6: thousandths	7: tens thousandths

✍ *Round each decimal number to the nearest place indicated.*

1) 0.2̲3̲
   0.2

2) 4.0̲4
   4.0

3) 5.6̲23
   5.6

4) 0.2̲66
   0.3

5) 6̲.37
   6

6) 0.8̲8
   0.9

7) 8.2̲4
   8.2

8) 7̲.0760
   7

9) 1.6̲29
   1.63

10) 6.3̲959
    6.4

11) 1̲.9
    2

12) 5̲.2167
    5

13) 5.8̲63
    5.9

14) 8.5̲4
    8.5

15) 80.6̲9
    81

16) 65.8̲5
    66

17) 70.7̲8
    70.8

18) 615.7̲55
    616

19) 16̲.4
    16

20) 95̲.81
    96

21) 2̲.408
    2

22) 76̲.3
    76

23) 116.5̲14
    116.5

24) 8.0̲6
    8.1

Adding and Subtracting Decimals

Helpful	1– Line up the numbers.	Example:
	2– Add zeros to have same number of digits for both numbers.	16.18
Hints		− 13.45
	3– Add or Subtract using column addition or subtraction.	2.73

✎**Add and subtract decimals.**

1)
$$\begin{array}{r} {}^{4\,10\,{}^{14}}\!\!15.14 \\ -\ 12.18 \\ \hline 2.96 \end{array}$$

3)
$$\begin{array}{r} {}^{1}82.56 \\ +\ 12.28 \\ \hline 94.84 \end{array}$$

5)
$$\begin{array}{r} {}^{,\,\,\backslash}90.37 \\ +\ 56.97 \\ \hline 147.34 \end{array}$$

2)
$$\begin{array}{r} {}^{\backslash}65.72 \\ +\ 43.67 \\ \hline 109.39 \end{array}$$

4)
$$\begin{array}{r} {}^{3\ 11}34.18 \\ -\ 23.45 \\ \hline 10.73 \end{array}$$

6)
$$\begin{array}{r} {}^{6\ 18}45.78 \\ -\ 23.39 \\ \hline 22.39 \end{array}$$

✎**Solve.**

7) $\underline{3.5} + 1.3 = 4.8$

10) $6.9 + \underline{9.5} = 16.4$

8) $4.2 + \underline{7.4} = 11.6$

11) $\underline{3.5} + 5.1 = 8.6$

9) $9.9 + \underline{6.1} = 16$

12) $\underline{7.3} + 7.9 = 15.2$

Multiplying and Dividing Decimals

Helpful *Hints*	**For Multiplication:** – Set up and multiply the numbers as you do with whole numbers. – Count the total number of decimal places in both of the factors. – Place the decimal point in the product. **For Division:** – If the divisor is not a whole number, move decimal point to right to make it a whole number. Do the same for dividend. – Divide similar to whole numbers.

✍ *Find each product.*

1) $\begin{array}{r} 4.5 \\ \times\ 1.6 \\ \hline 7.2 \end{array}$

2) $\begin{array}{r} 7.7 \\ \times\ 9.9 \\ \hline 76.23 \end{array}$

3) $\begin{array}{r} 2.6 \\ \times\ 1.5 \\ \hline 3.9 \end{array}$

4) $\begin{array}{r} 8.9 \\ \times\ 9.7 \\ \hline 86.33 \end{array}$

5) $\begin{array}{r} 15.1 \\ \times\ 12.6 \\ \hline 190.26 \end{array}$

6) $\begin{array}{r} 6.9 \\ \times\ 3.3 \\ \hline 22.77 \end{array}$

7) $\begin{array}{r} 5.7 \\ \times\ 7.8 \\ \hline 44.46 \end{array}$

8) $\begin{array}{r} 98.20 \\ \times\ 100 \\ \hline 9820 \end{array}$

9) $\begin{array}{r} 23.99 \\ \times\ 1000 \\ \hline 23990 \end{array}$

✍ *Find each quotient.*

10) $9.2 \div 3.6$ 2.55

11) $27.6 \div 3.8$ 7.263

12) $12.6 \div 4.7$

13) $6.5 \div 8.1$ .802

14) $1.4 \div 10$ .14

15) $3.6 \div 100$ .036

16) $4.24 \div 10$ .424

17) $14.6 \div 100$ .146

18) $1.8 \div 1000$ .0018

Converting Between Fractions, Decimals and Mixed Numbers

Helpful	**Fraction to Decimal:**
	– Divide the top number by the bottom number.
Hints	**Decimal to Fraction:**
	– Write decimal over 1.
	– Multiply both top and bottom by 10 for every digit on the right side of the decimal point.
	– Simplify.

✎ **Convert fractions to decimals.**

1) $\frac{9}{10}$ = .9

2) $\frac{56}{100}$ = .56

3) $\frac{3}{4}$ = .75

4) $\frac{2}{5}$ = .4

5) $\frac{3}{9}$ = .333...

6) $\frac{40}{50}$ = .8

7) $\frac{12}{10}$ = 1.2

8) $\frac{8}{5}$ = 1.6

9) $\frac{69}{10}$ = 6.9

✎ **Convert decimal into fraction or mixed numbers.**

10) 0.3 $\frac{3}{10}$

11) 4.5 $4\frac{1}{2}$

12) 2.5 $2\frac{1}{2}$

13) 2.3 $2\frac{3}{10}$

14) 0.8 $\frac{4}{5}$

15) 0.25 $\frac{1}{4}$

16) 0.14 $\frac{7}{50}$

17) 0.2 $\frac{1}{5}$

18) 0.08 $\frac{2}{25}$

19) 0.45 $\frac{9}{20}$

20) 2.6 $2\frac{3}{5}$

21) 5.2 $5\frac{1}{5}$

Factoring Numbers

Helpful	-	Factoring numbers means to break the numbers into their prime factors.	**Example:**
Hints	-	First few prime numbers: 2, 3, 5, 7, 11, 13, 17, 19	$12 = 2 \times 2 \times 3$

✍ List all positive factors of each number.

1) 68
1,2,4,17,34,68

2) 56
1,2,4,7,8,14,28,56

3) 24
1,2,3,4,6,8,12,24

4) 40
1,2,4,5,8,10,20,40

5) 86
1,2,43,86

6) 78
1,2,3,6,13,26,39,78

7) 50
1,2,5,10,25,50

8) 98
1,2,7,14,49,98

9) 45
1,3,5,9,15,45

10) 26
1,2,13,26

11) 54
1,2,3,6,9,18,27,54

12) 28
1,2,4,7,14,28

13) 55
1,5,11,55

14) 85
1,5,17,85

15) 48
1,2,3,4,6,8,12,16,24,48

✍ List the prime factorization for each number.

16) 50
$2 \times 5 \times 5$

17) 25
5×5

18) 69
3×23

19) 21
3×7

20) 45
$3 \times 3 \times 5$

21) 68
$2 \times 2 \times 17$

22) 26
2×13

23) 86
2×43

24) 93
3×31

Greatest Common Factor

Helpful	- List the prime factors of each number. - Multiply common prime factors.	**Example:**
Hints		$200 = 2 \times 2 \times 2 \times 5 \times 5$ $60 = 2 \times 2 \times 3 \times 5$ GCF $(200, 60) = 2 \times 2 \times 5 = 20$

✎*Find the GCF for each number pair.*

1) 20, 30
⑩ $2 \times 2 \times 5$
   $2 \times 3 \times 5$

2) 4, 14
② 2×2
   2×7

3) 5, 45
⑤ 5
   $3 \times 3 \times 5$

4) 68, 12
④ $2 \times 2 \times 17$
   $2 \times 2 \times 6$

5) 5, 12
① 5
   $2 \times 2 \times 3$

6) 15, 27
③ 3×5
   $3 \times 3 \times 3$

7) 3, 24
③ 3
   $2 \times 2 \times 2 \times 3$

8) 34, 6
② 2×17
   2×3

9) 4, 10
② 2×2
   2×5

10) 5, 3
①

11) 6, 16
② 2×3
   $2 \times 2 \times 2 \times 2$

12) 30, 3
③

13) 24, 28
④ $2 \times 2 \times 2 \times 3$
   $2 \times 2 \times 7$

14) 70, 10
⑩ $2 \times 5 \times 7$
   2×5

15) 45, 8
① $3 \times 3 \times 5$
   $2 \times 2 \times 2$

16) 90, 35
⑤ $2 \times 3 \times 3 \times 5$
   5×7

17) 78, 34
② $2 \times 3 \times 13$
   2×17

18) 55, 75
⑤ 5×11
   $3 \times 5 \times 5$

19) 60, 72
⑫ $2 \times 2 \times 3 \times 5$
   $2 \times 2 \times 2 \times 3 \times 3$

20) 100, 78
② $2 \times 2 \times 5 \times 5$
   $2 \times 3 \times 13$

21) 30, 40
⑩ $2 \times 3 \times 5$
   $2 \times 2 \times 2 \times 5$

26

Least Common Multiple

Helpful *Hints*	- Find the GCF for the two numbers. - Divide that GCF into either number. - Take that answer and multiply it by the other number.	**Example:** LCM (200, 60): GCF is 20 200 ÷ 20 = 10 10 × 60 = 600

✎ *Find the LCM for each number pair.*

1) 4, 14

(28)   4÷2=2
       2×14=28

2) 5, 15

(15)   5÷5=1
       1×15=15

3) 16, 10

(80) 16÷2=8
      10×8=80

4) 4, 34

(68)   4÷2=2
       34×2=68

5) 8, 3

(24)

6) 12, 24

(24)

7) 9, 18

(18)

8) 5, 6

(30)

9) 8, 19

(152)   ⁷19
        ×8
        ___
        152

10) 9, 21

(63)   9÷3=3
       3×21=63

11) 19, 29

(481) ¹19
       ×29
       ___
       01
       38
       ___
       481

12) 7, 6

(42)

13) 25, 6

(150)

14) 4, 8

(8)

15) 30, 10, 50

16) 18, 36, 27

17) 12, 8, 18

18) 8, 18, 4

19) 26, 20, 30

20) 10, 4, 24

21) 15, 30, 45

Answers of Worksheets – CHAPTER 1

Simplifying Fractions

1) $\dfrac{11}{18}$

2) $\dfrac{4}{5}$

3) $\dfrac{2}{3}$

4) $\dfrac{3}{4}$

5) $\dfrac{1}{3}$

6) $\dfrac{1}{4}$

7) $\dfrac{4}{9}$

8) $\dfrac{1}{2}$

9) $\dfrac{2}{5}$

10) $\dfrac{1}{9}$

11) $\dfrac{5}{9}$

12) $\dfrac{3}{4}$

13) $\dfrac{5}{8}$

14) $\dfrac{13}{16}$

15) $\dfrac{1}{5}$

16) $\dfrac{4}{7}$

17) $\dfrac{1}{2}$

18) $\dfrac{5}{12}$

19) $\dfrac{3}{8}$

20) $\dfrac{1}{4}$

21) $\dfrac{5}{9}$

Adding and Subtracting Fractions

1) $\dfrac{7}{6}$

2) $\dfrac{14}{15}$

3) $\dfrac{4}{3}$

4) $\dfrac{83}{36}$

5) $\dfrac{3}{5}$

6) $\dfrac{13}{14}$

7) $\dfrac{23}{20}$

8) $\dfrac{13}{15}$

9) $\dfrac{31}{25}$

10) $\dfrac{2}{5}$

11) $\dfrac{11}{35}$

12) $\dfrac{1}{6}$

13) $\dfrac{13}{45}$

14) $\dfrac{3}{14}$

15) $\dfrac{1}{6}$

16) $\dfrac{1}{36}$

17) $\dfrac{9}{40}$

18) $\dfrac{7}{18}$

Multiplying and Dividing Fractions

1) $\dfrac{2}{15}$

2) $\dfrac{1}{2}$

3) $\dfrac{6}{35}$

4) $\dfrac{1}{8}$

5) $\dfrac{6}{25}$

6) $\dfrac{7}{27}$

7) $\dfrac{1}{4}$

8) $\dfrac{1}{12}$

9) $\dfrac{5}{12}$

10) $\dfrac{8}{9}$

11) $\dfrac{3}{2}$

12) $\dfrac{8}{11}$

13) $\dfrac{55}{7}$

14) $\dfrac{27}{25}$

15) 1

16) 3

17) $\dfrac{4}{3}$

18) $\dfrac{25}{63}$

Adding Mixed Numbers

1) 10

2) $5\dfrac{1}{2}$

3) $10\dfrac{4}{5}$

4) 4

5) $10\dfrac{2}{3}$

6) $4\dfrac{2}{3}$

7) $3\dfrac{8}{33}$

8) 4

9) $10\dfrac{4}{5}$

10) $7\dfrac{1}{5}$

11) $2\dfrac{1}{21}$

12) $3\dfrac{3}{4}$

Subtract Mixed Numbers

1) 1

2) $\dfrac{1}{4}$

3) $1\dfrac{2}{5}$

4) $\dfrac{2}{3}$

5) $\dfrac{2}{3}$

6) 2

7) $1\dfrac{19}{33}$

8) 1

9) $4\dfrac{2}{5}$

10) $6\dfrac{1}{5}$

11) $1\dfrac{8}{21}$

12) $\dfrac{3}{4}$

Multiplying Mixed Numbers

1) $2\frac{1}{12}$

2) $2\frac{2}{3}$

3) $5\frac{10}{21}$

4) $5\frac{31}{40}$

5) $7\frac{17}{25}$

6) $2\frac{2}{9}$

7) $4\frac{1}{16}$

8) $7\frac{12}{25}$

9) $11\frac{1}{3}$

10) $3\frac{9}{10}$

11) $1\frac{2}{3}$

12) $4\frac{2}{25}$

Dividing Mixed Numbers

1) $\frac{22}{25}$

2) $1\frac{19}{20}$

3) $\frac{19}{28}$

4) $\frac{1}{2}$

5) $1\frac{13}{20}$

6) $1\frac{9}{26}$

7) $2\frac{34}{63}$

8) $1\frac{11}{20}$

9) $2\frac{2}{15}$

10) $1\frac{34}{35}$

11) $3\frac{7}{10}$

12) 2

Comparing Decimals

1) $1.25 < 2.3$

2) $0.5 > 0.23$

3) $3.2 = 3.2$

4) $4.58 < 45.8$

5) $2.75 > 0.275$

6) $5.2 > 5$

7) $3.1 > 0.31$

8) $6.33 > 0.733$

9) $8 > 0.8$

10) $4.56 > 0.456$

11) $1.12 < 1.14$

12) $2.77 < 2.78$

13) $6.08 < 6.11$

14) $1.11 > 0.211$

15) $2.6 > 2.55$

16) $1.24 < 1.25$

17) $5.52 > 0.552$

18) $0.33 > 0.033$

19) $14.4 = 14.4$

20) $0.05 < 0.50$

21) $0.59 < 0.7$

22) $0.3 > 0.03$

23) $0.90 = 0.9$

24) $0.27 < 0.4$

Rounding Decimals

1) 0.2
2) 4.0
3) 5.6
4) 0.3
5) 6
6) 0.9
7) 8.2
8) 7

9) 1.63
10) 6.4
11) 2
12) 5
13) 5.9
14) 8.5
15) 81
16) 66

17) 70.8
18) 616
19) 16
20) 96
21) 2
22) 76
23) 116.5
24) 8.1

Adding and Subtracting Decimals

1) 2.96
2) 109.39
3) 94.84
4) 10.73

5) 147.34
6) 22.39
7) 3.5
8) 7.4

9) 6.1
10) 9.5
11) 3.5
12) 7.3

Multiplying and Dividing Decimals

1) 7.2
2) 76.23
3) 3.9
4) 86.33
5) 190.26
6) 22.77

7) 44.46
8) 9820
9) 23990
10) 2.5555…
11) 7.2631…
12) 2.6808…

13) 0.8024…
14) 0.14
15) 0.036
16) 0.424
17) 0.146
18) 0.0018

Converting Between Fractions, Decimals and Mixed Numbers

1) 0.9
2) 0.56
3) 0.75
4) 0.4
5) 0.333…
6) 0.8

7) 1.2
8) 1.6
9) 6.9
10) $\frac{3}{10}$
11) $4\frac{1}{2}$

12) $2\frac{1}{2}$
13) $2\frac{3}{10}$
14) $\frac{4}{5}$
15) $\frac{1}{4}$

16) $\frac{7}{50}$ 18) $\frac{2}{25}$ 20) $2\frac{3}{5}$

17) $\frac{1}{5}$ 19) $\frac{9}{20}$ 21) $5\frac{1}{5}$

Factoring Numbers

1) 1, 2, 4, 17, 34, 68
2) 1, 2, 4, 7, 8, 14, 28, 56
3) 1, 2, 3, 4, 6, 8, 12, 24
4) 1, 2, 4, 5, 8, 10, 20, 40
5) 1, 2, 43, 86
6) 1, 2, 3, 6, 13, 26, 39, 78
7) 1, 2, 5, 10, 25, 50
8) 1, 2, 7, 14, 49, 98
9) 1, 3, 5, 9, 15, 45
10) 1, 2, 13, 26
11) 1, 2, 3, 6, 9, 18, 27, 54
12) 1, 2, 4, 7, 14, 28

13) 1, 5, 11, 55
14) 1, 5, 17, 85
15) 1, 2, 3, 4, 6, 8, 12, 16, 24, 48
16) $2 \times 5 \times 5$
17) 5×5
18) 3×23
19) 3×7
20) $3 \times 3 \times 5$
21) $2 \times 2 \times 17$
22) 2×13
23) 2×43
24) 3×31

Greatest Common Factor

1) 10
2) 2
3) 5
4) 4
5) 1
6) 3
7) 3

8) 2
9) 2
10) 1
11) 2
12) 3
13) 4
14) 10

15) 1
16) 5
17) 2
18) 5
19) 12
20) 2
21) 10

Least Common Multiple

1) 28
2) 15
3) 80
4) 68
5) 24
6) 24
7) 18

8) 30
9) 152
10) 63
11) 551
12) 42
13) 150
14) 8

15) 150
16) 108
17) 72
18) 72
19) 780
20) 120
21) 90

Chapter 2: Real Numbers and Integers

Math Topics that you'll learn today:

✓ Adding and Subtracting Integers

✓ Multiplying and Dividing Integers

✓ Ordering Integers and Numbers

✓ Arrange and Order, Comparing Integers

✓ Order of Operations

✓ Mixed Integer Computations

✓ Integers and Absolute Value

"Wherever there is number, there is beauty." –Proclus

Adding and Subtracting Integers

Helpful	-	**Integers:** {... , –3, –2, –1, 0, 1, 2, 3, ...} Includes: zero, counting numbers, and the negative of the counting numbers.	**Example:**
		– Add a positive integer by moving to the right on the number line.	12 + 10 = 22
Hints			25 – 13 = 12
		– Add a negative integer by moving to the left on the number line.	(–24) + 12 = –12
			(–14) + (–12) = –26
		– Subtract an integer by adding its opposite.	14 – (–13) = 27

✎ *Find the sum.*

1) (– 12) + (– 4)

    -16

2) 5 + (– 24)

    -19

3) (– 14) + 23

    9

4) (– 8) + 39

    31

5) 43 + (–12)

    31

6) (– 23) + (– 4) + 3

    -24

7) 4 + (– 12) + (– 10) + (– 25)

    -43

8) 19 + (– 15) + 25 + 11

    40

9) (– 9) + (– 12) + (32 – 14)

    -3

10) 4 + (– 30) + (45 – 34)

    -15

✎ *Find the difference.*

11) (– 14) – (– 9) – (18)

12) (– 9) – (– 25)

13) (– 12) – (8)

14) (28) – (– 4)

15) (34) – (2)

16) (55) – (– 5) + (– 4)

17) (9) – (2) – (– 5)

18) (2) – (4) – (– 15)

19) (23) – (4) – (– 34)

20) (– 45) – (– 87)

Multiplying and Dividing Integers

Helpful *Hints*	(negative) × (negative) = positive	**Examples:**
	(negative) ÷ (negative) = positive	$3 \times 2 = 6$
	(negative) × (positive) = negative	$3 \times -3 = -9$
	(negative) ÷ (positive) = negative	$-2 \times -2 = 4$
	(positive) × (positive) = positive	$10 \div 2 = 5$
		$-4 \div 2 = -2$
		$-12 \div -6 = 3$

✍ *Find each product.*

1) $(-8) \times (-2)$

2) 3×6

3) $(-4) \times 5 \times (-6)$

4) $2 \times (-6) \times (-6)$

5) $11 \times (-12)$

6) $10 \times (-5)$

7) 8×8

8) $(-8) \times (-9)$

9) $6 \times (-5) \times 3$

10) $6 \times (-1) \times 2$

✍ *Find each quotient.*

11) $18 \div 3$

12) $(-24) \div 4$

13) $(-63) \div (-9)$

14) $54 \div 9$

15) $20 \div (-2)$

16) $(-66) \div (-11)$

17) $64 \div 8$

18) $(-121) \div 11$

19) $72 \div 9$

20) $16 \div 4$

Ordering Integers and Numbers

Helpful *Hints*	To compare numbers, you can use number line! As you move from left to right on the number line, you find a bigger number!	**Example:** Order integers from least to greatest. $(-11, -13, 7, -2, 12)$ $-13 < -11 < -2 < 7 < 12$

✎ *Order each set of integers from least to greatest.*

1) $-15, -19, 20, -4, 1$ ___, ___, ___, ___, ___, ___

2) $6, -5, 4, -3, 2$ ___, ___, ___, ___, ___, ___

3) $15, -42, 19, 0, -22$ ___, ___, ___, ___, ___, ___

4) $26, -91, 0, -13, 67, -55$ ___, ___, ___, ___, ___, ___

5) $-17, -71, 90, -25, -54, -39$ ___, ___, ___, ___, ___, ___

6) $98, 5, 46, 19, 77, 24$ ___, ___, ___, ___, ___, ___

✎ *Order each set of integers from greatest to least.*

7) $-2, 5, -3, 6, -4$ ___, ___, ___, ___, ___, ___

8) $-37, 7, -17, 27, 47$ ___, ___, ___, ___, ___, ___

9) $32, -27, 19, -17, 15$ ___, ___, ___, ___, ___, ___

10) $68, 81, 21, -18, 94, 72$ ___, ___, ___, ___, ___, ___

Arrange, Order, and Comparing Integers

Helpful *Hints*	When using a number line, numbers increase as you move to the right.	**Examples:** $5 < 7,$ $-5 < -2$ $-18 < -12$

✎**Arrange these integers in descending order.**

1) 21, 71, − 18, − 10, 82   ___, ___, ___, ___, ___, ___

2) 15, 11, 20, 12, − 9, − 5   ___, ___, ___, ___, ___, ___

3) − 5, 20, 15, 9, −11   ___, ___, ___, ___, ___, ___

4) 19, 18, − 9, − 6, − 11   ___, ___, ___, ___, ___, ___

5) 56, − 34, − 12, − 5, 32   ___, ___, ___, ___, ___, ___

✎**Compare. Use >, =, <**

6) − 8 _____ 12   11) − 56 _____ − 58

7) − 10 _____ −16   12) 78 _____ 87

8) 43 _____ 34   13) − 92 _____ − 102

9) 15 _____ −16   14) − 12 _____ − 12

10) − 354 _____ −345   15) − 721 _____ − 821

Order of Operations

Helpful	-	Use "order of operations" rule when there are more than one math operation.	**Example:**
Hints	-	PEMDAS (parentheses / exponents / multiply / divide / add / subtract)	$(12 + 4) \div (-4) = -4$

✎ *Evaluate each expression.*

1) $(2 \times 2) + 5$

2) $24 - (3 \times 3)$

3) $(6 \times 4) + 8$

4) $25 - (4 \times 2)$

5) $(6 \times 5) + 3$

6) $64 - (2 \times 4)$

7) $25 + (1 \times 8)$

8) $(6 \times 7) + 7$

9) $48 \div (4 + 4)$

10) $(7 + 11) \div (-2)$

11) $9 + (2 \times 5) + 10$

12) $(5 + 8) \times \dfrac{3}{5} + 2$

13) $2 \times 7 - (\dfrac{10}{9 - 4})$

14) $(12 + 2 - 5) \times 7 - 1$

15) $(\dfrac{7}{5 - 1}) \times (2 + 6) \times 2$

16) $20 \div (4 - (10 - 8))$

17) $\dfrac{50}{4 \, (5 - 4) - 3}$

18) $2 + (8 \times 2)$

Mixed Integer Computations

Helpful *Hints*	**It worth remembering:** (negative) × (negative) = positive (negative) ÷ (negative) = positive (negative) × (positive) = negative (negative) ÷ (positive) = negative (positive) × (positive) = positive	**Example:** (−5) + 6 = 1 (−3) × (−2) = 6 (9) ÷ (−3) = − 3

✎ *Compute.*

1) $(-70) \div (-5)$

2) $(-14) \times 3$

3) $(-4) \times (-15)$

4) $(-65) \div 5$

5) $18 \times (-7)$

6) $(-12) \times (-2)$

7) $\dfrac{(-60)}{(-20)}$

8) $24 \div (-8)$

9) $22 \div (-11)$

10) $\dfrac{(-27)}{3}$

11) $4 \times (-4)$

12) $\dfrac{(-48)}{12}$

13) $(-14) \times (-2)$

14) $(-7) \times (7)$

15) $\dfrac{-30}{-6}$

16) $(-54) \div 6$

17) $(-60) \div (-5)$

18) $(-7) \times (-12)$

19) $(-14) \times 5$

20) $88 \div (-8)$

Integers and Absolute Value

Helpful Hints	To find an absolute value of a number, just find it's distance from 0!	Example:
		$\lvert -6 \rvert = 6$
		$\lvert 6 \rvert = 6$
		$\lvert -12 \rvert = 12$
		$\lvert 12 \rvert = 12$

✎ **Write absolute value of each number.**

1) -4

2) -7

3) -8

4) 4

5) 5

6) -10

7) 1

8) 6

9) 8

10) -2

11) -1

12) 10

13) 3

14) 7

15) -5

16) -3

17) -9

18) 2

19) 4

20) -6

21) 9

✎ **Evaluate.**

22) $\lvert -43 \rvert - \lvert 12 \rvert + 10$

23) $76 + \lvert -15 - 45 \rvert - \lvert 3 \rvert$

24) $30 + \lvert -62 \rvert - 46$

25) $\lvert 32 \rvert - \lvert -78 \rvert + 90$

26) $\lvert -35 + 4 \rvert + 6 - 4$

27) $\lvert -4 \rvert + \lvert -11 \rvert$

28) $\lvert -6 + 3 - 4 \rvert + \lvert 7 + 7 \rvert$

29) $\lvert -9 \rvert + \lvert -19 \rvert - 5$

Answers of Worksheets – CHAPTER 2

Adding and Subtracting Integers

1) -16	8) 40	15) 32
2) -19	9) -3	16) 56
3) 9	10) -15	17) 12
4) 31	11) -23	18) 13
5) 31	12) 16	19) 53
6) -24	13) -20	20) 42
7) -43	14) 32	

Multiplying and Dividing Integers

1) 16	8) 72	15) -10
2) 18	9) -90	16) 6
3) 120	10) -12	17) 8
4) 72	11) 6	18) -11
5) -132	12) -6	19) 8
6) -50	13) 7	20) 4
7) 64	14) 6	

Ordering Integers and Numbers

1) $-19, -15, -4, 1, 20$	6) $5, 19, 24, 46, 77, 98$
2) $-5, -3, 2, 4, 6$	7) $6, 5, -2, -3, -4$
3) $-42, -22, 0, 15, 19$	8) $47, 27, 7, -17, -37$
4) $-91, -55, -13, 0, 26, 67$	9) $32, 19, 15, -17, -27$
5) $-71, -54, -39, -25, -17, 90$	10) $94, 81, 72, 68, 21, -18$

Arrange and Order, Comparing Integers

1) $82, 71, 21, -10, -18$

2) $20, 15, 12, 11, -5, -9$

3) $20, 15, 9, -5, -11$

4) $19, 18, -6, -9, -11$

5) $56, 32, -5, -12, -34$

6) $<$

7) $>$

8) $>$

9) $>$

10) $<$

11) $>$

12) $<$

13) $>$

14) $=$

15) $>$

Order of Operations

1) 9

2) 15

3) 32

4) 17

5) 33

6) 56

7) 33

8) 49

9) 6

10) -9

11) 29

12) 9.8

13) 12

14) 62

15) 28

16) 10

17) 50

18) 18

Mixed Integer Computations

1) 14

2) -42

3) 60

4) -13

5) -126

6) 24

7) 3

8) -3

9) -2

10) -9

11) -16

12) -4

13) 28

14) -49

15) 5

16) -9

17) 12

18) 84

19) -70

20) -11

Integers and Absolute Value

1) 4	11) 1	21) 9
2) 7	12) 10	22) 41
3) 8	13) 3	23) 133
4) 4	14) 7	24) 46
5) 5	15) 5	25) 44
6) 10	16) 3	26) 33
7) 1	17) 9	27) 15
8) 6	18) 2	28) 21
9) 8	19) 4	29) 23
10) 2	20) 6	

Chapter 3: Proportions and Ratios

Math Topics that you'll learn today:

- ✓ Writing Ratios
- ✓ Simplifying Ratios
- ✓ Create a Proportion
- ✓ Similar Figures
- ✓ Simple Interest
- ✓ Ratio and Rates Word Problems

"Do not worry about your difficulties in mathematics. I can assure you mine are still greater." – Albert Einstein

Writing Ratios

Helpful	– A ratio is a comparison of two numbers. Ratio can be written as a division.	Example:
Hints		$3:5$, or $\frac{3}{5}$

✎ *Express each ratio as a rate and unite rate.*

1) 12 miles on 4 gallons of gas.

2) 24 dollars for 6 books.

3) 200 miles on 14 gallons of gas

4) 24 inches of snow in 8 hours

✎ *Express each ratio as a fraction in the simplest form.*

5) 3 feet out of 30 feet

6) 18 cakes out of 42 cakes

7) 16 dimes t0 24 dimes

8) 12 dimes out of 48 coins

9) 14 cups to 84 cups

10) 45 gallons to 65 gallons

11) 10 miles out of 40 miles

12) 22 blue cars out of 55 cars

13) 32 pennies to 300 pennies

14) 24 beetles out of 86 insects

Simplifying Ratios

Helpful *Hints*	– You can calculate equivalent ratios by multiplying or dividing both sides of the ratio by the same number.	**Examples:** 3 : 6 = 1 : 2 4 : 9 = 8 : 18

✎*Reduce each ratio.*

1) 21 : 49

2) 20 : 40

3) 10 : 50

4) 14 : 18

5) 45 : 27

6) 49 : 21

7) 100 : 10

8) 12 : 8

9) 35 : 45

10) 8 : 20

11) 25 : 35

12) 21 : 27

13) 52 : 82

14) 12 : 36

15) 24 : 3

16) 15 : 30

17) 3 : 36

18) 8 : 16

19) 6 : 100

20) 2 : 20

21) 10 : 60

22) 14 : 63

23) 68 : 80

24) 8 : 80

Create a Proportion

Helpful	– A proportion contains 2 equal fractions! A proportion simply means that two fractions are equal.	**Example:**
Hints		2, 4, 8, 16
		$\dfrac{2}{4} = \dfrac{8}{16}$

✎*Create proportion from the given set of numbers.*

1) 1, 6, 2, 3

2) 12, 144, 1, 12

3) 16, 4, 8, 2

4) 9, 5, 27, 15

5) 7, 10, 60, 42

6) 8, 7, 24, 21

7) 10, 5, 8, 4

8) 3, 12, 8, 2

9) 2, 2, 1, 4

10) 3, 6, 7, 14

11) 2, 6, 5, 15

12) 7, 2, 14, 4

Similar Figures

Helpful Hints	– Two or more figures are similar if the corresponding angles are equal, and the corresponding sides are in proportion.	**Example:** 3–4–5 triangle is similar to a 6–8–10 triangle

✎*Each pair of figures is similar. Find the missing side.*

1)

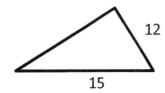 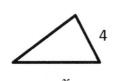

2)

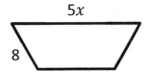 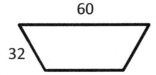

3)

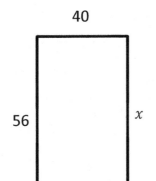 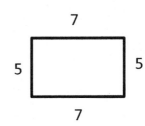

Simple Interest

Helpful	**Simple Interest:** The charge for borrowing money or the return for lending it. Interest = principal x rate x time	**Example:**
Hints	$$I = prt$$	$450 at 7% for 8 years. $$I = prt$$ $$I = 450 \times 0.07 \times 8 = \$252 =$$

✎**Use simple interest to find the ending balance.**

1) $ 1,300 at 5% for 6 years

2) $ 5,400 at 7.5% for $\frac{1}{2}$ year

3) $ 25,600 at 9.2% for 5 years

4) $ 24,000 at 8.5% for 9 years

5) $ 240 interest is earned on a principal of $ 1500 at a simple interest rate of 4% pa. For how many years was the principal invested?

6) A new car, valued at $ 28,000, depreciates at 9% per year. Find the value of the car 3 years after purchase.

7) Joe bought a car for $ 12,400 on the following terms: 15% deposit, 18% simple interest, repayments made monthly for 2 years. How much was the deposit?

Ratio and Rates Word Problems

Helpful	To solve a ratio or a rate word problem, create a proportion and use cross multiplication method!	**Example:**
Hints		$\dfrac{x}{4} = \dfrac{8}{16}$
		$16x = 4 \times 8$
		$x = 2$

✍️ *Solve.*

1) In a party, 10 soft drinks are required for every 12 guests. If there are 252 guests, how many soft drink is required?

2) In Jack's class, 18 of the students are tall and 10 are short. In Michael's class 54 students are tall and 30 students are short. Which class has a higher ratio of tall to short students?

3) Are these ratios equivalent?

   12 cards to 72 animals 11 marbles to 66 marbles

4) The price of 3 apples at the Quick Market is $1.44. The price of 5 of the same apples at Walmart is $2.50. Which place is the better buy?

5) The bakers at a Bakery can make 160 bagels in 4 hours. How many bagels can they bake in 16 hours? What is that rate per hour?

6) You can buy 5 cans of green beans at a supermarket for $3.40. How much does it cost to buy 35 cans of green beans?

Answers of Worksheets – Chapter 3

Writing Ratios

1) $\frac{120 \ miles}{4 \ gallons}$, 30 miles per gallon

2) $\frac{24 \ dollars}{6 \ books}$, 4.00 dollars per book

3) $\frac{200 \ miles}{14 \ gallons}$, 14.29 miles per gallon

4) $\frac{24" \ of \ snow}{8 \ hou}$, 3 inches of snow per hour

5) $\frac{1}{10}$

6) $\frac{3}{7}$

7) $\frac{2}{3}$

8) $\frac{1}{4}$

9) $\frac{1}{6}$

10) $\frac{9}{13}$

11) $\frac{1}{4}$

12) $\frac{2}{5}$

13) $\frac{8}{75}$

14) $\frac{12}{43}$

Simplifying Ratios

1) 3 : 7
2) 1 : 2
3) 1 : 5
4) 7 : 9
5) 5 : 3
6) 7 : 3
7) 10 : 1
8) 3 : 2

9) 7 : 9
10) 2 : 5
11) 5 : 7
12) 7 : 9
13) 26 : 41
14) 1 : 3
15) 8 : 1
16) 1 : 2

17) 1 : 12
18) 1 : 2
19) 3 : 50
20) 1 : 10
21) 1: 6
22) 2 : 9
23) 17 : 20
24) 1 : 10

Create a Proportion

1) 1 : 3 = 2 : 6

2) 12 : 144 = 1 : 12

3) 2 : 4 = 8 : 16

4) 5 : 15 = 9 : 27

5) 7 : 42, 10 : 60

6) 7 : 21 = 8 : 24

7) 8 : 10 = 4 : 5

8) 2 : 3 = 8 : 12

9) 4 : 2 = 2 : 1

10) 7 : 3 = 14 : 6   11) 5 : 2 = 15 : 6   12) 7 : 2 = 14 : 4

Similar Figures

1) 5   2) 3   3) 56

Simple Interest

1) $ 390   4) $ 18,360   7) $1860

2) $ 202.5   5) 4

3) $ 11,776   6) $ 20,440

Ratio and Rates Word Problems

1) 210

2) The ratio for both class is equal to 9 to 5.

3) Yes! Both ratios are 1 to 6

4) The price at the Quick Market is a better buy.

5) 640, the rate is 40 per hour.

6) $23.80

Chapter 4: Percent

Math Topics that you'll learn today:

- ✓ Percentage Calculations
- ✓ Converting Between Percent, Fractions, and Decimals
- ✓ Percent Problems
- ✓ Markup, Discount, and Tax

"Do not worry about your difficulties in mathematics. I can assure you mine are still greater." –
Albert Einstein

Percentage Calculations

| *Helpful* | - | Use the following formula to find part, whole, or percent: | **Example:** |
| *Hints* | | $part = \dfrac{percent}{100} \times whole$ | $\dfrac{20}{100} \times 100 = 20$ |

✎ *Calculate the percentages.*

1) 50% of 25

2) 80% of 15

3) 30% of 34

4) 70% of 45

5) 10% of 0

6) 80% of 22

7) 65% of 8

8) 78% of 54

9) 50% of 80

10) 20% of 10

11) 40% of 40

12) 90% of 0

13) 20% of 70

14) 55% of 60

15) 80% of 10

16) 20% of 880

17) 70% of 100

18) 80% of 90

✎ *Solve.*

19) 50 is what percentage of 75?

20) What percentage of 100 is 70

21) Find what percentage of 60 is 35.

22) 40 is what percentage of 80?

Converting Between Percent, Fractions, and Decimals

Helpful	– To a percent: Move the decimal point 2 places to the right and add the % symbol.	**Examples:**
Hints	– Divide by 100 to convert a number from percent to decimal.	30% = 0.3
		0.24 = 24%

✎ *Converting fractions to decimals.*

1) $\dfrac{50}{100}$

2) $\dfrac{38}{100}$

3) $\dfrac{15}{100}$

4) $\dfrac{80}{100}$

5) $\dfrac{7}{100}$

6) $\dfrac{35}{100}$

7) $\dfrac{90}{100}$

8) $\dfrac{20}{100}$

9) $\dfrac{7}{100}$

✎ *Write each decimal as a percent.*

10) 0.5

11) 0.9

12) 0.002

13) 0.524

14) 0.1

15) 0.03

16) 3.63

17) 0.008

18) 4.78

Percent Problems

Helpful	Base = Part ÷ Percent	**Example:**
	Part = Percent × Base	2 is 10% of 20.
Hints	Percent = Part ÷ Base	$2 \div 0.10 = 20$
		$2 = 0.10 \times 20$
		$0.10 = 2 \div 20$

✎ *Solve each problem.*

1) 51 is 340% of what?

2) 93% of what number is 97?

3) 27% of 142 is what number?

4) What percent of 125 is 29.3?

5) 60 is what percent of 126?

6) 67 is 67% of what?

7) 67 is 13% of what?

8) 41% of 78 is what?

9) 1 is what percent of 52.6?

10) What is 59% of 14 m?

11) What is 90% of 130 inches?

12) 16 inches is 35% of what?

13) 90% of 54.4 hours is what?

14) What percent of 33.5 is 21?

15) Liam scored 22 out of 30 marks in Algebra, 35 out of 40 marks in science and 89 out of 100 marks in mathematics. In which subject his percentage of marks in best?

16) Ella require 50% to pass. If she gets 280 marks and falls short by 20 marks, what were the maximum marks she could have got?

Markup, Discount, and Tax

		Example:
Helpful	- **Markup** = selling price – cost Markup rate = markup divided by the cost	
Hints	- **Discount:** Multiply the regular price by the rate of discount	Original price of a microphone: $49.99, discount: 5%, tax: 5%
	Selling price = original price – discount	
	- **Tax:** To find tax, multiply the tax rate to the taxable amount (income, property value, etc.)	Selling price = 49.87

✎ *Find the selling price of each item.*

1) Cost of a pen: $1.95, markup: 70%, discount: 40%, tax: 5%

2) Cost of a puppy: $349.99, markup: 41%, discount: 23%

3) Cost of a shirt: $14.95, markup: 25%, discount: 45%

4) Cost of an oil change: $21.95, markup: 95%

5) Cost of computer: $1,850.00, markup: 75%

Answers of Worksheets – Chapter 4

Percentage Calculations

1) 12.5	9) 40	17) 70
2) 12	10) 2	18) 72
3) 10.2	11) 16	19) 67%
4) 31.5	12) 0	20) 70%
5) 0	13) 14	21) 58%
6) 17.6	14) 33	22) 50%
7) 5.2	15) 8	
8) 42.12	16) 176	

Converting Between Percent, Fractions, and Decimals

1) 0.5	7) 0.9	13) 52.4%
2) 0.38	8) 0.2	14) 10%
3) 0.15	9) 0.07	15) 3%
4) 0.8	10) 50%	16) 363%
5) 0.07	11) 90%	17) 0.8%
6) 0.35	12) 0.2%	18) 478%

Percent Problems

1) 15	7) 515.4	13) 49 hours
2) 104.3	8) 31.98	14) 62.7%
3) 38.34	9) 1.9%	15) Mathematics
4) 23.44%	10) 8.3 m	16) 600
5) 47.6%	11) 117 inches	
6) 100	12) 45.7inches	

Markup, Discount, and Tax

1) $2.09

2) $379.98

3) $10.28

4) $36.22

5) $3,237.50

Chapter 5: Algebraic Expressions

Math Topics that you'll learn today:

- ✓ Expressions and Variables
- ✓ Simplifying Variable Expressions
- ✓ Simplifying Polynomial Expressions
- ✓ Translate Phrases into an Algebraic Statement
- ✓ The Distributive Property
- ✓ Evaluating One Variable
- ✓ Evaluating Two Variables
- ✓ Combining like Terms

Without mathematics, there's nothing you can do. Everything around you is mathematics. Everything around you is numbers." – Shakuntala Devi

Expressions and Variables

Helpful	A variable is a letter that represents unknown numbers. A variable can be used in the same manner as all other numbers:	
Hints	Addition	$2 + a$	2 plus a
	Subtraction	$y - 3$	y minus 3
	Division	$\dfrac{4}{x}$	4 divided by x
	Multiplication	$5a$	5 times a

✎ *Simplify each expression.*

1) $x + 5x$,

   use $x = 5$

2) $8(-3x + 9) + 6$,

   use $x = 6$

3) $10x - 2x + 6 - 5$,

   use $x = 5$

4) $2x - 3x - 9$,

   use $x = 7$

5) $(-6)(-2x - 4y)$,

   use $x = 1$, $y = 3$

6) $8x + 2 + 4y$,

   use x = 9, $y = 2$

7) $(-6)(-8x - 9y)$,

   use $x = 5$, $y = 5$

8) $6x + 5y$,

   use $x = 7$, $y = 4$

✎ *Simplify each expression.*

9) $5(-4 + 2x)$

10) $-3 - 5x - 6x + 9$

11) $6x - 3x - 8 + 10$

12) $(-8)(6x - 4) + 12$

13) $9(7x + 4) + 6x$

14) $(-9)(-5x + 2)$

Simplifying Variable Expressions

Helpful	– Combine "like" terms. (values with same variable and same power)	**Example:**
Hints	– Use distributive property if necessary.	$2x + 2\,(1 - 5x) =$
		$2x + 2 - 10x = -8x + 2$
	Distributive Property:	
	$a\,(b\,+\,c)\,=\,ab\,+\,ac$	

✎ *Simplify each expression.*

1) $-2 - x^2 - 6x^2$

2) $3 + 10x^2 + 2$

3) $8x^2 + 6x + 7x^2$

4) $5x^2 - 12x^2 + 8x$

5) $2x^2 - 2x - x$

6) $(-6)\,(8x - 4)$

7) $4x + 6\,(2 - 5x)$

8) $10x + 8\,(10x - 6)$

9) $9\,(-2x - 6) - 5$

10) $3\,(x + 9)$

11) $7x + 3 - 3x$

12) $2.5x^2 \times (-8x)$

✎ *Simplify.*

13) $-2(4 - 6x) - 3x,\ x = 1$

14) $2x + 8x,\ x = 2$

15) $9 - 2x + 5x + 2,\ x = 5$

16) $5\,(3x + 7),\ x = 3$

17) $2\,(3 - 2x) - 4,\ x = 6$

18) $5x + 3x - 8,\ x = 3$

19) $x - 7x,\ x = 8$

20) $5\,(-2 - 9x),\ x = 4$

Simplifying Polynomial Expressions

Helpful	-	In mathematics, a polynomial is an expression consisting of variables and coefficients that involves only the operations of addition, subtraction, multiplication, and non–negative integer exponents of variables.	**Example:**
Hints		$$P(x) = a_0x^n + a_1x^{n-1} + ... + a_{n-2}2x^2 + a_{n-1}x + a_n$$	An example of a polynomial of a single indeterminate x is $x^2 - 4x + 7$. An example for three variables is $x^3 + 2xyz^2 - yz + 1$

✎*Simplify each polynomial.*

1) $4x^5 - 5x^6 + 15x^5 - 12x^6 + 3x^6$

2) $(-3x^5 + 12 - 4x) + (8x^4 + 5x + 5x^5)$

3) $10x^2 - 5x^4 + 14x^3 - 20x^4 + 15x^3 - 8x^4$

4) $-6x^2 + 5x^2 - 7x^3 + 12 + 22$

5) $12x^5 - 5x^3 + 8x^2 - 8x^5$

6) $5x^3 + 1 + x^2 - 2x - 10x$

7) $14x^2 - 6x^3 - 2x(4x^2 + 2x)$

8) $(4x^4 - 2x) - (4x - 2x^4)$

9) $(3x^2 + 1) - (4 + 2x^2)$

10) $(2x + 2) - (7x + 6)$

11) $(12x^3 + 4x^4) - (2x^4 - 6x^3)$

12) $(12 + 3x^3) + (6x^3 + 6)$

13) $(5x^2 - 3) + (2x^2 - 3x^3)$

14) $(23x^3 - 12x^2) - (2x^2 - 9x^3)$

15) $(4x - 3x^3) - (3x^3 + 4x)$

Translate Phrases into an Algebraic Statement

Helpful *Hints*	**Translating key words and phrases into algebraic expressions:** **Addition:** plus, more than, the sum of, etc. **Subtraction:** minus, less than, decreased, etc. **Multiplication:** times, product, multiplied, etc. **Division:** quotient, divided, ratio, etc. **Example:** eight more than a number is 20 $8 + x = 20$

✎ *Write an algebraic expression for each phrase.*

1) A number increased by forty–two.

2) The sum of fifteen and a number

3) The difference between fifty–six and a number.

4) The quotient of thirty and a number.

5) Twice a number decreased by 25.

6) Four times the sum of a number and − 12.

7) A number divided by − 20.

8) The quotient of 60 and the product of a number and − 5.

9) Ten subtracted from a number.

10) The difference of six and a number.

The Distributive Property

Helpful	Distributive Property:	Example:
Hints	$a\,(b\,+\,c)\,=\,ab\,+\,ac$	$3\,(4\,+\,3x)$ $=\,12\,+\,9x$

✎ **Use the distributive property to simply each expression.**

1) $-(-2-5x)$

2) $(-6x+2)(-1)$

3) $(-5)\,(x-2)$

4) $-(7-3x)$

5) $8\,(8+2x)$

6) $2\,(12+2x)$

7) $(-6x+8)\,4$

8) $(3-6x)(-7)$

9) $(-12)\,(2x+1)$

10) $(8-2x)\,9$

11) $(-2x)\,(-1+9x)-4x\,(4+5x)$

12) $3\,(-5x-3)+4(6-3x)$

13) $(-2)(x+4)-(2+3x)$

14) $(-4)(3x-2)+6\,(x+1)$

15) $(-5)(4x-1)+4\,(x+2)$

16) $(-3)(x+4)-(2+3x)$

Evaluating One Variable

Helpful	– To evaluate one variable expression, find the variable and substitute a number for that variable.	**Example:**
Hints	– Perform the arithmetic operations.	$4x + 8, x = 6$ $4(6) + 8 = 24 + 8 = 32$

✎ *Simplify each algebraic expression.*

1) $9 - x$, $x = 3$

2) $x + 2$, $x = 5$

3) $3x + 7$, $x = 6$

4) $x + (-5)$, $x = -2$

5) $3x + 6$, $x = 4$

6) $4x + 6$, $x = -1$

7) $10 + 2x - 6$, $x = 3$

8) $10 - 3x$, $x = 8$

9) $\frac{20}{x} - 3$, $x = 5$

10) $(-3) + \frac{x}{4} + 2x$, $x = 16$

11) $(-2) + \frac{x}{7}$, $x = 21$

12) $(-\frac{14}{x}) - 9 + 4x$, $x = 2$

13) $(-\frac{6}{x}) - 9 + 2x$, $x = 3$

14) $(-2) + \frac{x}{8}$, $x = 16$

15) $8(5x - 12)$, $x = -2$

Evaluating Two Variables

Helpful	To evaluate an algebraic expression, substitute a number for each variable and perform the arithmetic operations.	**Example:**
Hints		$2x + 4y - 3 + 2,$
		$x = 5, y = 3$
		$2(5) + 4(3) - 3 + 2$
		$= 10$
		$+ 12 - 3 + 2$
		$= 21$

✍ *Simplify each algebraic expression.*

1) $2x + 4y - 3 + 2,$

 $x = 5, y = 3$

2) $(-\dfrac{12}{x}) + 1 + 5y,$

 $x = 6, y = 8$

3) $(-4)(-2a - 2b),$

 $a = 5, b = 3$

4) $10 + 3x + 7 - 2y,$

 $x = 7, y = 6$

5) $9x + 2 - 4y,$

 $x = 7, y = 5$

6) $6 + 3(-2x - 3y),$

 $x = 9, y = 7$

7) $12x + y,$

 $x = 4, y = 8$

8) $x \times 4 \div y,$

 $x = 3, y = 2$

9) $2x + 14 + 4y,$

 $x = 6, y = 8$

10) $4a - (5 - b),$

 $a = 4, b = 6$

Combining like Terms

Helpful	– Terms are separated by "+" and "−" signs.	**Example:**
Hints	– Like terms are terms with same variables and same powers.	$22x + 6 + 2x =$
	– Be sure to use the "+" or "−" that is in front of the coefficient.	$24x + 6$

✎*Simplify each expression.*

1) $5 + 2x - 8$

2) $(-2x + 6)\,2$

3) $7 + 3x + 6x - 4$

4) $(-4) - (3)(5x + 8)$

5) $9x - 7x - 5$

6) $x - 12x$

7) $7\,(3x + 6) + 2x$

8) $(-11x) - 10x$

9) $3x - 12 - 5x$

10) $13 + 4x - 5$

11) $(-22x) + 8x$

12) $2\,(4 + 3x) - 7x$

13) $(-4x) - (6 - 14x)$

14) $5\,(6x - 1) + 12x$

15) $22x + 6 + 2x$

16) $(-13x) - 14x$

17) $(-6x) - 9 + 15x$

18) $(-6x) + 7x$

19) $(-5x) + 12 + 7x$

20) $(-3x) - 9 + 15x$

21) $20x - 19x$

Answers of Worksheets – Chapter 5

Expressions and Variables

1) 30
2) −66
3) 41
4) −16
5) 84

6) 82
7) 510
8) 62
9) $10x − 20$
10) $6 − 11x$

11) $3x + 2$
12) $44 − 48x$
13) $69x + 36$
14) $45x − 18$

Simplifying Variable Expressions

1) $− 7x^2 − 2$
2) $10x^2 + 5$
3) $15x^2 + 6x$
4) $− 7x^2 + 8x$
5) $2x^2 − 3x$
6) $− 48x + 24$
7) $− 26x + 12$

8) $90x − 48$
9) $− 18x − 59$
10) $3x + 27$
11) $4x + 3$
12) $− 20x^3$
13) 1
14) 20

15) 26
16) 80
17) $− 22$
18) 16
19) $− 48$
20) $− 190$

Simplifying Polynomial Expressions

1) $− 14x^6 + 19x^5$
2) $2x^5 + 8x^4 + x + 12$
3) $−33x^4 + 29x^3 + 10x^2$
4) $−7x^3 − x^2 + 34$
5) $4x^5 − 5x^3 + 8x^2$
6) $5x^3 + x^2 − 12x + 1$
7) $−14x^3 + 10x^2$
8) $6x^4 − 6x$

9) $x^2 − 3$
10) $− 5x − 4$
11) $2x^4 + 18x^3$
12) $9x^3 + 18$
13) $−3x^3 + 7x^2 − 3$
14) $32x^3 − 14x^2$
15) $−6x^3$

Translate Phrases into an Algebraic Statement

1) $X + 42$
3) $56 − x$
4) $30/x$
5) $2x − 25$
8) $\dfrac{60}{−5x}$

2) $15 + x$
6) $4(x + (−12))$
7) $\dfrac{x}{−20}$
9) $x − 10$
10) $6 − x$

The Distributive Property

1) 5x + 2	7) − 24x + 32	13) − 5x − 10
2) 6x − 2	8) 42x − 21	14) − 6x + 14
3) −5x + 10	9) − 24x − 12	15) − 16x + 13
4) 3x − 7	10) − 18x + 72	16) − 6x − 14
5) 16x + 64	11) − 38x^2 − 14x	
6) 4x + 24	12) − 27x + 15	

Evaluating One Variable

1) 6	6) 2	11) 1
2) 7	7) 10	12) −8
3) 25	8) −14	13) −5
4) −7	9) 1	14) 0
5) 18	10) 33	15) −176

Evaluating Two Variables

1) 21	5) 45	9) 58
2) 39	6) −111	10) 17
3) 64	7) 56	
4) 26	8) 6	

Combining like Terms

1) 2x − 3	8) −21x	15) 24x + 6
2) −4x + 12	9) −2x − 12	16) −27x
3) 9x + 3	10) 4x + 8	17) 9x − 9
4) −15x − 28	11) −14x	18) x
5) 2x − 5	12) − x + 8	19) 2x + 12
6) −11x	13) 10x − 6	20) 12x − 9
7) 23x + 42	14) 42x − 5	21) x

Chapter 6: Equations

Math Topics that you'll learn today:

- ✓ One– Step Equations
- ✓ Two– Step Equations
- ✓ Multi– Step Equations

"The study of mathematics, like the Nile, begins in minuteness but ends in magnificence."

– Charles Caleb Colton

One–Step Equations

Helpful	-	The values of two expressions on both sides of an equation are equal.	**Example:**
		$ax + b = c$	$-8x = 16$
Hints	-	You only need to perform one Math operation in order to solve the equation.	$x = -2$

✍ *Solve each equation.*

1) $x + 3 = 17$

2) $22 = (-8) + x$

3) $3x = (-30)$

4) $(-36) = (-6x)$

5) $(-6) = 4 + x$

6) $2 + x = (-2)$

7) $20x = (-220)$

8) $18 = x + 5$

9) $(-23) + x = (-19)$

10) $5x = (-45)$

11) $x - 12 = (-25)$

12) $x - 3 = (-12)$

13) $(-35) = x - 27$

14) $8 = 2x$

15) $(-6x) = 36$

16) $(-55) = (-5x)$

17) $x - 30 = 20$

18) $8x = 32$

19) $36 = (-4x)$

20) $4x = 68$

21) $30x = 300$

Two–Step Equations

Helpful	– You only need to perform two math operations (add, subtract, multiply, or divide) to solve the equation.	**Example:**
Hints	– Simplify using the inverse of addition or subtraction.	$- 2\,(x - 1) = 42$ $(x - 1) = - 21$ $x = - 20$
	– Simplify further by using the inverse of multiplication or division.	

✎ *Solve each equation.*

1) $5\,(8 + x) = 20$
  $x = -4$

2) $(- 7)\,(x - 9) = 42$
  $x = 3$

3) $(- 12)\,(2x - 3) = (- 12)$
  $x = 2$

4) $6\,(1 + x) = 12$
  $x = 1$

5) $12\,(2x + 4) = 60$
  $x = .5$

6) $7\,(3x + 2) = 42$
  $x = 1.333...$

7) $8\,(14 + 2x) = (- 34)$
  $x = -9$

8) $(- 15)\,(2x - 4) = 48$
  $x = -6.6$

9) $3\,(x + 5) = 12$
  $x = -1$

10) $\dfrac{3x - 12}{6} = 4$
  $x = 12$

11) $(- 12) = \dfrac{x + 15}{6}$
  $x = -87$

12) $110 = (- 5)(2x - 6)$
  $x = -14$

13) $\dfrac{x}{8} - 12 = 4$
  $x = 128$

14) $20 = 12 + \dfrac{x}{4}$
  $x = 32$

15) $\dfrac{- 24 + x}{6} = (- 12)$
  $x = -48$

16) $(- 4)\,(5 + 2x) = (- 100)$
  $x = 10$

17) $(- 12x) + 20 = 32$
  $x = -1$

18) $\dfrac{-2 + 6x}{4} = (- 8)$

19) $\dfrac{x + 6}{5} = (- 5)$

20) $(- 9) + \dfrac{x}{4} = (- 15)$

Multi–Step Equations

Helpful	– Combine "like" terms on one side.	**Example:**
	– Bring variables to one side by adding or subtracting.	$3x + 15 = -2x + 5$
Hints		Add 2x both sides
	– Simplify using the inverse of addition or subtraction.	$5x + 15 = +5$
		Subtract 15 both sides
	– Simplify further by using the inverse of multiplication or division.	$5x = -10$
		Divide by 5 both sides
		$x = -2$

✍ *Solve each equation.*

1) $-(2 - 2x) = 10$

2) $-12 = -(2x + 8)$

3) $3x + 15 = (-2x) + 5$

4) $-28 = (-2x) - 12x$

5) $2(1 + 2x) + 2x = -118$

6) $3x - 18 = 22 + x - 3 + x$

7) $12 - 2x = (-32) - x + x$

8) $7 - 3x - 3x = 3 - 3x$

9) $6 + 10x + 3x = (-30) + 4x$

10) $(-3x) - 8(-1 + 5x) = 352$

11) $24 = (-4x) - 8 + 8$

12) $9 = 2x - 7 + 6x$

13) $6(1 + 6x) = 294$

14) $-10 = (-4x) - 6x$

15) $4x - 2 = (-7) + 5x$

16) $5x - 14 = 8x + 4$

17) $40 = -(4x - 8)$

18) $(-18) - 6x = 6(1 + 3x)$

19) $x - 5 = -2(6 + 3x)$

20) $6 = 1 - 2x + 5$

Answers of Worksheets – Chapter 6

One–Step Equations

1) 14
2) 30
3) − 10
4) 6
5) − 10
6) − 4
7) − 11

8) 13
9) 4
10) − 9
11) − 13
12) − 9
13) − 8
14) 4

15) − 6
16) 11
17) 50
18) 4
19) − 9
20) 17
21) 10

Two–Step Equations

1) − 4
2) 3
3) 2
4) 1
5) 0.5
6) $\frac{4}{3}$
7) $-\frac{73}{8}$

8) $\frac{2}{5}$
9) − 1
10) 12
11) − 87
12) − 8
13) 128
14) 32

15) − 48
16) 10
17) − 1
18) − 5
19) − 31
20) − 24

Multi–Step Equations

1) 6
2) 2
3) − 2
4) 2
5) − 20
6) 37
7) 22

8) $\frac{4}{3}$
9) − 4
10) − 8
11) − 6
12) 2
13) 8

14) 1
15) 5
16) − 6
17) − 8
18) − 1
19) − 1
20) 0

Chapter 7: Inequalities

Math Topics that you'll learn today:

- ✓ Graphing Single– Variable Inequalities
- ✓ One– Step Inequalities
- ✓ Two– Step Inequalities
- ✓ Multi– Step Inequalities

Without mathematics, there's nothing you can do. Everything around you is mathematics. Everything around you is numbers." – Shakuntala Devi

Graphing Single–Variable Inequalities

Helpful	– Isolate the variable.
	– Find the value of the inequality on the number line.
Hints	– For less than or greater than draw open circle on the value of the variable.
	– If there is an equal sign too, then use filled circle.
	– Draw a line to the right direction.

✍*Draw a graph for each inequality.*

1) $-2 > x$

2) $5 \leq -x$

3) $x > 7$

4) $-x > 1.5$

One–Step Inequalities

Helpful *Hints*	– Isolate the variable. – For dividing both sides by negative numbers, flip the direction of the inequality sign.	**Example:** $x + 4 \geq 11$ $x \geq 7$

✎*Solve each inequality and graph it.*

1) $x + 9 \geq 11$

2) $x - 4 \leq 2$

3) $6x \geq 36$

4) $7 + x < 16$

5) $x + 8 \leq 1$

6) $3x > 12$

7) $3x < 24$

Two–Step Inequalities

Helpful *Hints*	– Isolate the variable. – For dividing both sides by negative numbers, flip the direction of the of the inequality sign. – Simplify using the inverse of addition or subtraction. – Simplify further by using the inverse of multiplication or division.	**Example:** $2x + 9 \geq 11$ $2x \geq 2$ $x \geq 1$

✎ *Solve each inequality and graph it.*

1) $3x - 4 \leq 5$

2) $2x - 2 \leq 6$

3) $4x - 4 \leq 8$

4) $3x + 6 \geq 12$

5) $6x - 5 \geq 19$

6) $2x - 4 \leq 6$

7) $8x - 4 \leq 4$

8) $6x + 4 \leq 10$

9) $5x + 4 \leq 9$

10) $7x - 4 \leq 3$

11) $4x - 19 < 19$

12) $2x - 3 < 21$

13) $7 + 4x \geq 19$

14) $9 + 4x < 21$

15) $3 + 2x \geq 19$

16) $6 + 4x < 22$

Multi–Step Inequalities

Helpful *Hints*	– Isolate the variable. – Simplify using the inverse of addition or subtraction. – Simplify further by using the inverse of multiplication or division.	**Example:** $\dfrac{7x + 1}{3} \geq 5$ $7x + 1 \geq 15$ $7x \geq 14$ $x \geq 7$

✎ *Solve each inequality.*

1) $\dfrac{9x}{7} - 7 < 2$

2) $\dfrac{4x + 8}{2} \leq 12$

3) $\dfrac{3x - 8}{7} > 1$

4) $-3\,(x - 7) > 21$

5) $4 + \dfrac{x}{3} < 7$

6) $\dfrac{2x + 6}{4} \leq 10$

Answers of Worksheets – Chapter 7

Graphing Single–Variable Inequalities

1) $-2 > x$

2) $x \leq -5$

3) $x > 7$

4) $-1.5 > x$

One–Step Inequalities

1) $x + 9 \geq 11$

2) $x - 4 \leq 2$

3) $6x \geq 36$

4) $7 + x < 16$

5) $x + 8 \leq 1$

6) $3x > 12$

7) $3x < 24$

Two–Step inequalities

1) $x \leq 3$

2) $x \leq 4$

3) $x \leq 3$

4) $x \geq 2$

5) $x \geq 4$

6) $x \leq 5$

7) $x \leq 1$

8) $x \leq 1$

9) $x \leq 1$

10) $x \leq 1$

11) $x < 9.5$

12) $x < 12$

13) $x \geq 3$

14) $x < 3$

15) $x \geq 8$

16) $x < 4$

Multi–Step inequalities

1) $x < 7$

2) $x \leq 4$

3) $x > 5$

4) $x < 0$

5) $x < 9$

6) $x \leq 17$

Chapter 8: Linear Functions

Math Topics that you'll learn today:

- ✓ Finding Slope
- ✓ Graphing Lines Using Slope– Intercept Form
- ✓ Graphing Lines Using Standard Form
- ✓ Writing Linear Equations
- ✓ Graphing Linear Inequalities
- ✓ Finding Midpoint
- ✓ Finding Distance of Two Points

"Sometimes the questions are complicated and the answers are simple." – Dr. Seuss

Finding Slope

Helpful	Slope of a line:		Example:
Hints		$\dfrac{y_2 - y_1}{x_2 - x_1} = \dfrac{rise}{run}$	$(2, -10), (3, 6)$ slope = 16

✍ *Find the slope of the line through each pair of points.*

1) $(1, 1), (3, 5)$

2) $(4, -6), (-3, -8)$

3) $(7, -12), (5, 10)$

4) $(19, 3), (20, 3)$

5) $(15, 8), (-17, 9)$

6) $(6, -12), (15, -3)$

7) $(3, 1), (7, -5)$

8) $(3, -2), (-7, 8)$

9) $(15, -3), (-9, 5)$

10) $(-4, 7), (-6, -4)$

11) $(6, -8), (-11, -7)$

12) $(-6, 13), (17, -9)$

13) $(-10, -2), (-6, -5)$

14) $(4, 5), (-4, 10)$

15) $(-3, 1), (-17, 2)$

16) $(7, 0), (-13, -11)$

17) $(17, -13), (17, 8)$

18) $(12, 2), (-7, 5)$

Graphing Lines Using Slope–Intercept Form

Helpful	**Slope–intercept form:** given the slope *m* and the y–intercept *b*, then the equation of the line is:
Hints	$y = mx + b$.

Example:

$y = 8x - 3$

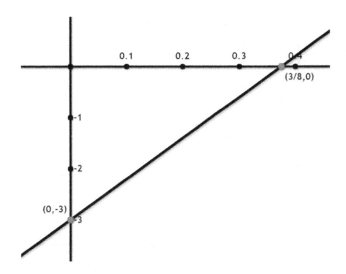

✍️ **Sketch the graph of each line.**

1)

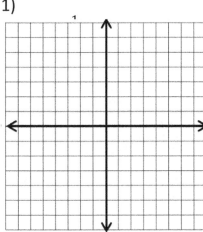

2)

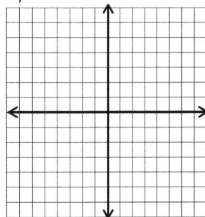

Graphing Lines Using Standard Form

Helpful	– Find the –intercept of the line by putting zero for y.
Hints	– Find the y–intercept of the line by putting zero for the x.
	– Connect these two points.

Example:

$x + 4y = 12$

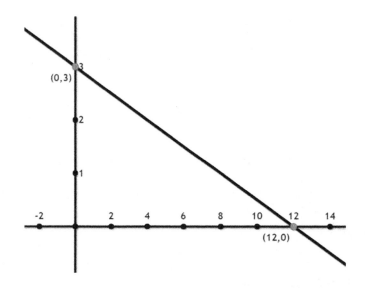

 Sketch the graph of each line.

1)

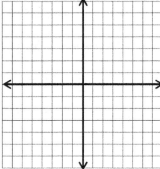

2)

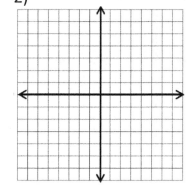

Writing Linear Equations

| *Helpful* *Hints* | The equation of a line:

$$y = mx + b$$

1– Identify the slope.

2– Find the y–intercept. This can be done by substituting the slope and the coordinates of a point (x, y) on the line. | **Example:**

through:

$(-4, -2), (-3, 5)$

$y = 7x + 26$ |

✍ *Write the slope–intercept form of the equation of the line through the given points.*

1) through: $(-4, -2), (-3, 5)$

2) through: $(5, 4), (-4, 3)$

3) through: $(0, -2), (-5, 3)$

4) through: $(-1, 1), (-2, 6)$

5) through: $(0, 3), (-4, -1)$

6) through: $(0, 2), (1, -3)$

7) through: $(0, -5), (4, 3)$

8) through: $(-1, 4), (0, 4)$

9) through: $(2, -3), (3, -5)$

10) through: $(2, 5), (-1, -4)$

11) through: $(1, -3), (-3, 1)$

12) through: $(3, 3), (1, -5)$

13) through: $(4, 4), (3, -5)$

14) through: $(0, 3), (1, 1)$

15) through: $(5, 5), (2, -3)$

16) through: $(-2, -2), (2, -5)$

17) through: $(-3, -2), (1, -1)$

18) through: $(-2, 1), (6, 5)$

Graphing Linear Inequalities

Helpful *Hints*	1– First, graph the "equals" line.
	2– Choose a testing point. (it can be any point on both sides of the line.)
	3– Put the value of (x, y) of that point in the inequality. If that works, that part of the line is the solution. If the values don't work, then the other part of the line is the solution.

 Sketch the graph of each linear inequality.

1)

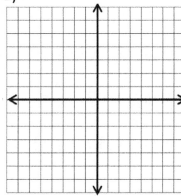

2)

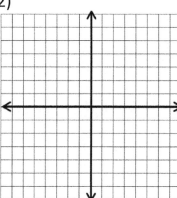

4)

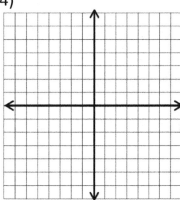

5)

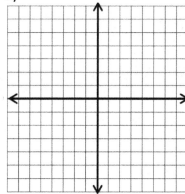

Finding Midpoint

Helpful Hints	Midpoint of the segment AB: $M\left(\dfrac{x_1+x_2}{2}, \dfrac{y_1+y_2}{2}\right)$	Example: (3, 9), (− 1, 6) M (1, 7.5)

✍ *Find the midpoint of the line segment with the given endpoints.*

1) (5, 4), (− 3, 8)

2) (2, − 2), (3, − 5)

3) (− 2, 6), (− 3, − 2)

4) (0, 2), (− 2, − 6)

5) (7, 4), (9, − 1)

6) (4, − 5), (0, 8)

7) (1, − 2), (1, − 6)

8) (− 2, − 3), (3, − 6)

9) (7, 0), (− 7, 5)

10) (− 2, 6), (− 3, − 2)

11) (− 1, 1), (5, − 5)

12) (2.3, − 1.3), (− 2.2, − 0.5)

13) (4.1, 6.32), (4, 5.6)

14) (2, − 1), (− 6, 0)

15) (− 4, 4), (5, − 1)

16) (− 2, − 3), (− 6, 5)

17) $(\frac{1}{2}, 1)$, (2, 4)

18) (− 2, − 2), (6, 5)

Finding Distance of Two Points

Helpful *Hints*	Distance from A to B: $$d = \sqrt{(x_1 - x_2)^2 + (y_1 - y_2)^2}$$	**Example:** $(-1, 2), (-1, -7)$ Distance = 9

✎ **Find the distance between each pair of points.**

1) $(-1, 2), (-1, -7)$

2) $(6, 4), (-1, 3)$

3) $(-8, -5), (-6, 1)$

4) $(-6, -10), (-2, -10)$

5) $(4, -6), (-3, 4)$

6) $(-6, -7), (-2, -8)$

7) $(5, 4), (8, 2)$

8) $(8, 4), (3, -7)$

9) $(1, 3), (5, 7)$

10) $(4, 2), (-7, 1)$

11) $(-3, -4), (-7, -2)$

12) $(-7, -2), (6, 9)$

13) $(10, 0), (0, 4)$

14) $(-3, 2), (5, 0)$

15) $(-5, 6), (8, -4)$

16) $(3, -5), (-8, -4)$

17) $(0, 8), (4, 10)$

18) $(6, 4), (-5, -1)$

Answers of Worksheets – Chapter 8

Finding Slope

1) 2

2) $\dfrac{2}{7}$

3) −11

4) 0

5) $-\dfrac{1}{32}$

6) 1

7) $-\dfrac{3}{2}$

8) −1

9) $-\dfrac{1}{3}$

10) $\dfrac{11}{2}$

11) $-\dfrac{1}{17}$

12) $-\dfrac{22}{23}$

13) $-\dfrac{3}{4}$

14) $-\dfrac{5}{8}$

15) $-\dfrac{1}{14}$

16) $\dfrac{11}{20}$

17) Undefined

18) $-\dfrac{3}{19}$

Graphing Lines Using Slope–Intercept Form

1)

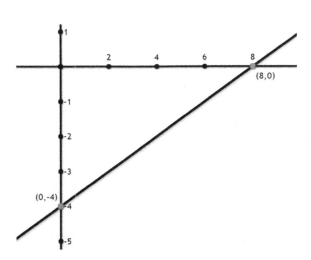

2)

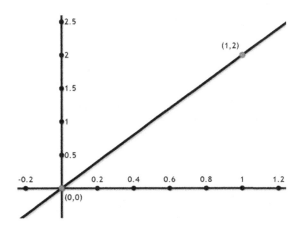

Graphing Lines Using Standard Form

1)

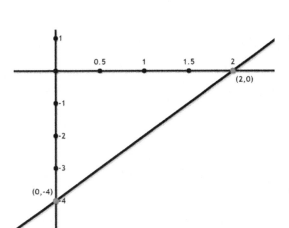

2)

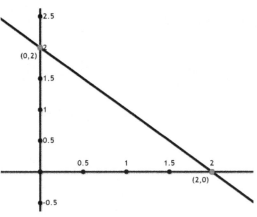

Writing Linear Equations

1) $y = 7x + 26$

2) $y = \frac{1}{9}x + \frac{31}{9}$

3) $y = -x - 2$

4) $y = -5x - 4$

5) $y = x + 3$

6) $y = -5x + 2$

7) $y = 2x - 5$

8) $y = 4$

9) $y = -2x + 1$

10) $y = 3x - 1$

11) $y = -x - 2$

12) $y = 4x - 9$

13) $y = 9x - 32$

14) $y = -2x + 3$

15) $y = \frac{8}{3}x - \frac{25}{3}$

16) $y = -\frac{3}{4}x - \frac{7}{2}$

17) $y = \frac{1}{4}x - \frac{5}{4}$

18) $y = -\frac{4}{3}x + \frac{19}{3}$

Graphing Linear Inequalities

1)

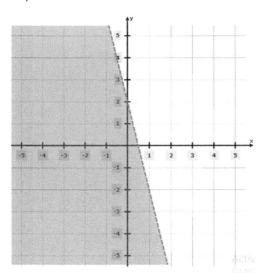

2)

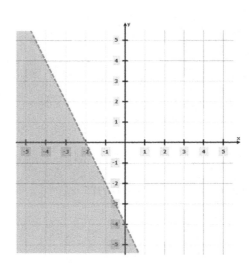

4)

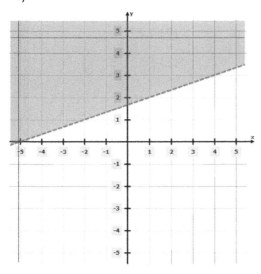

5)

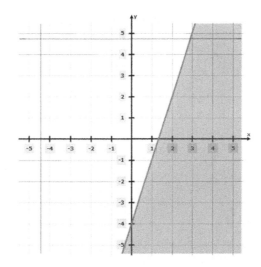

Finding Midpoint

1) (1, 6)
2) (2.5, −3.5)
3) (−2.5, 2)
4) (−1, −2)
5) (8, 1.5)
6) (2, 1.5)
7) (1, −4)

8) (0.5, −4.5)
9) (0, 2.5)
10) (−2.5, 2)
11) (2, −2)
12) (0.05, −0.9)
13) (4.05, 5.96)
14) (−2, − 0.5)

15) $(\frac{1}{2}, 1\frac{1}{2})$
16) (−4, 1)
17) (1.25, 2.5)
18) $(2, \frac{3}{2})$

Finding Distance of Two Points

1) 9
2) 7.1
3) 6.32
4) 4
5) 12.21
6) 4.12

7) 3.61
8) 12.1
9) 5.66
10) 11.04
11) 4.47
12) 17.03

13) 10.77
14) 8.25
15) 16.4
16) 10.3
17) 4.47
18) 12.1

Chapter 9: Polynomials

Math Topics that you'll learn today:

- ✓ Classifying Polynomials
- ✓ Writing Polynomials in Standard Form
- ✓ Simplifying Polynomials
- ✓ Adding and Subtracting Polynomials
- ✓ Multiplying Monomials
- ✓ Multiplying and Dividing Monomials
- ✓ Multiplying a Polynomial and a Monomial
- ✓ Multiplying Binomials
- ✓ Factoring Trinomials
- ✓ Operations with Polynomials

Mathematics – the unshaken Foundation of Sciences, and the plentiful Fountain of Advantage to human

affairs. — Isaac Barrow

Classifying Polynomials

	Name	Degree	Example
Helpful	constant	0	4
	linear	1	$2x$
Hints	quadratic	2	$x^2 + 5x + 6$
	cubic	3	$x^3 - x^2 + 4x + 8$
	quartic	4	$x^4 + 3x^3 - x^2 + 2x + 6$
	quantic	5	$x^5 - 2x^4 + x^3 - x^2 + x + 10$

✎*Name each polynomial by degree and number of terms.*

1) x

2) $-5x^4$

3) $7x - 4$

4) -6

5) $8x + 1$

6) $9x^2 - 8x^3$

7) $2x^5$

8) $10 + 8x$

9) $5x^2 - 6x$

10) $-7x^7 + 7x^4$

11) $-8x^4 + 5x^3 - 2x^2 - 8x$

12) $4x - 9x^2 + 4x^3 - 5x^4$

13) $4x^6 + 5x^5 + x^4$

14) $-4 - 2x^2 + 8x$

15) $9x^6 - 8$

16) $7x^5 + 10x^4 - 3x + 10x^7$

17) $4x^6 - 3x^2 - 8x^4$

18) $-5x^4 + 10x - 10$

Writing Polynomials in Standard Form

Helpful	A polynomial function $f(x)$ of degree n is of the form	**Example:**
Hints	$f(x) = a_n x^n + a_{n-1} x^{n-1} + \dots + a_1 x + a_0$	$2x^2 - 4x^3 - x =$
	The first term is the one with the biggest power!	$-4x^3 + 2x^2 - x$

✎ *Write each polynomial in standard form.*

1) $3x^2 - 5x^3$ $-5x^3 + 3x^2$

2) $3 + 4x^3 - 3$
  $4x^3$

3) $2x^2 + 1x - 6x^3$
  $-6x^3 + 2x^2 + 1x$

4) $9x - 7x$
  $2x$

5) $12 - 7x + 9x^4$
  $9x^4 - 7x + 12$

6) $5x^2 + 13x - 2x^3$
  $-2x^3 + 5x^2 + 13x$

7) $-3 + 16x - 16x$
  -3

8) $3x(x+4) - 2(x+4)$
  $3x^2 + 10x - 8$

9) $(x+5)(x-2)$
  $x^2 + 3x - 10$

10) $3x^2 + x + 12 - 5x^2 - 2x$
  $-2x^2 - x + 12$

11) $12x^5 + 7x^3 - 3x^5 - 8x^3$
  $9x^5 - x^3$

12) $3x(2x + 5 - 2x^2)$
  $-6x^3 + 6x^2 + 15x$

13) $11x(x^5 + 2x^3)$
  $11x^6 + 22x^4$

14) $(x+6)(x+3)$
  $x^2 + 9x + 18$

15) $(x+4)^2$ $x^2 + 4x + 4x +$
  $(x+4) \times (x+4)$ $\boxed{x^2 + 8x + 8}$

16) $(8x - 7)(3x + 2)$
  $24x^2 - 5x - 14$

17) $5x(3x^2 + 2x + 1)$
  $15x^3 + 10x^2 + 5x$

18) $7x(3 - x + 6x^3)$
  $42x^4 - 7x^2 + 21x$

√+
excellent
work!

Simplifying Polynomials

		Example:
Helpful	1– Find "like" terms. (they have same variables with same power).	
Hints	2– Add or Subtract "like" terms using PEMDAS operation.	$2x^5 - 3x^3 + 8x^2 - 2x^5 =$ $- 3x^3 + 8x^2$

✎ *Simplify each expression.*

1) $11 - 4x^2 + 3x^2 - 7x^3 + 3$

$(-7x^3 - x^2 + 8$

2) $2x^5 - x^3 + 8x^2 - 2x^5$

$-x^3 + 8x^2$

3) $(-5)(x^6 + 10) - 8(14 - x^6)$

$-13x^6 - 164$

4) $4(2x^2 + 4x^2 - 3x^3) + 6x^3 + 17$

$-18x^3 + 24x^2 + 17$

5) $11 - 6x^2 + 5x^2 - 12x^3 + 22$

$-12x^3 - 11x^2 - 11$

$2x^2 - 11x^2 - 11$

6) $2x^2 - 2x + 3x^3 + 12x - 22x$

7) $(3x - 8)(3x - 4)$

$9x^2 - 36x + 32$

8) $(12x + 2y)^2$

$(12x + 2y)(12x + 2y)$

$144x^2 + 24xy$

9) $(12x^3 + 28x^2 + 10x + 4) \div (x + 2)$

10) $(2x + 12x^2 - 2) \div (2x + 1)$

11) $(2x^3 - 1) + (3x^3 - 2x^3)$

12) $(x - 5)(x - 3)$

$x^2 - 8x - 15$

13) $(3x + 8)(3x - 8)$

$9x^2 - 64$

14) $(8x^2 - 3x) - (5x - 5 - 8x^2)$

Adding and Subtracting Polynomials

Helpful	Adding polynomials is just a matter of combining like terms, with some order of operations considerations thrown in.	**Example:**
Hints	Be careful with the minus signs, and don't confuse addition and multiplication!	$(3x^3 - 1) - (4x^3 + 2)$
		$= -x^3 - 3$

✎*Simplify each expression.*

1) $(2x^3 - 2) + (2x^3 + 2)$

2) $(4x^3 + 5) - (7 - 2x^3)$

3) $(4x^2 + 2x^3) - (2x^3 + 5)$

4) $(4x^2 - x) + (3x - 5x^2)$

5) $(7x + 9) - (3x + 9)$

6) $(4x^4 - 2x) - (6x - 2x^4)$

7) $(12x - 4x^3) - (8x^3 + 6x)$

8) $(2x^3 - 8x^2) - (5x^2 - 3x^3)$

9) $(2x^2 - 6) + (9x^2 - 4x^3)$

10) $(4x^3 + 3x^4) - (x^4 - 5x^3)$

11) $(-12x^4 + 10x^5 + 2x^3) + (14x^3 + 23x^5 + 8x^4)$

12) $(13x^2 - 6x^5 - 2x) - (-10x^2 - 11x^5 + 9x)$

13) $(35 + 9x^5 - 3x^2) + (8x^4 + 3x^5) - (27 - 5x^4)$

14) $(3x^5 - 2x^3 - 4x) + (4x + 10x^4 - 23) + (x^2 - x^3 + 12)$

Multiplying Monomials

Helpful	A monomial is a polynomial with just one term, like $2x$ or $7y$.	**Example:**
Hints		$2u^3 \times (-3u)$
		$= -6u^4$

✎ *Simplify each expression.*

1) $2xy^2z \times 4z^2$

2) $4xy \times x^2y$

3) $4pq^3 \times (-2p^4q)$

4) $8s^4t^2 \times st^5$

5) $12p^3 \times (-3p^4)$

6) $-4p^2q^3r \times 6pq^2r^3$

7) $(-8a^4) \times (-12a^6b)$

8) $3u^4v^2 \times (-7u^2v^3)$

9) $4u^3 \times (-2u)$

10) $-6xy^2 \times 3x^2y$

11) $12y^2z^3 \times (-y^2z)$

12) $5a^2bc^2 \times 2abc^2$

Multiplying and Dividing Monomials

Helpful	- When you divide two monomials you need to divide their coefficients and then divide their variables.
Hints	- In case of exponents with the same base, you need to subtract their powers.

Example:

$(-3x^2)(8x^4y^{12}) = -24x^6y^{12}$

$\dfrac{36\ x^5y^7}{4\ x^4y^5} = 9xy^2$

✑*Simplify.*

1) $(7x^4y^6)(4x^3y^4)$

2) $(15x^4)(3x^9)$

3) $(12x^2y^9)(7x^9y^{12})$

4) $\dfrac{80\ x^{12}y^9}{10\ x^6y^7}$

5) $\dfrac{95\ x^{18}y^7}{5\ x^9y^2}$

6) $\dfrac{200\ x^3y^8}{40\ x^3y^7}$

7) $\dfrac{-15\ x^{17}y^{13}}{3\ x^6y^9}$

8) $\dfrac{-64\ x^8y^{10}}{8\ x^3y^7}$

Multiplying a Polynomial and a Monomial

Helpful	– When multiplying monomials, use the product rule for exponents.	Example:
Hints	– When multiplying a monomial by a polynomial, use the distributive property.	$2x (8x - 2) =$
	$a \times (b + c) = a \times b + a \times c$	$16x^2 - 4x$

✎ *Find each product.*

1) $5 (3x - 6y)$

2) $9x (2x + 4y)$

3) $8x (7x - 4)$

4) $12x (3x + 9)$

5) $11x (2x - 11y)$

6) $2x (6x - 6y)$

7) $3x (2x^2 - 3x + 8)$

8) $13x (4x + 8y)$

9) $20 (2x^2 - 8x - 5)$

10) $3x (3x - 2)$

11) $6x^3 (3x^2 - 2x + 2)$

12) $8x^2 (3x^2 - 5xy + 7y^2)$

13) $2x^2 (3x^2 - 5x + 12)$

14) $2x^3 (2x^2 + 5x - 4)$

15) $5x (6x^2 - 5xy + 2y^2)$

16) $9 (x^2 + xy - 8y^2)$

Multiplying Binomials

Helpful	Use "FOIL". (First–Out–In–Last)	Example:
Hints	$(x + a)(x + b) = x^2 + (b + a)x + ab$	$(x + 2)(x - 3) =$ $x^2 - x - 6$

✎ *Multiply.*

1) $(3x - 2)(4x + 2)$

   $12x^2 + 14x - 4$

2) $(2x - 5)(x + 7)$

   $2x^2 + 19x - 35$

3) $(x + 2)(x + 8)$

   $x^2 + 10x + 16$

4) $(x^2 + 2)(x^2 - 2)$

   $x^4 + 4x^2 - 4$

5) $(x - 2)(x + 4)$

   $x^2 - 8x$

6) $(x - 8)(2x + 8)$

7) $(5x - 4)(3x + 3)$

8) $(x - 7)(x - 6)$

9) $(6x + 9)(4x + 9)$

10) $(2x - 6)(5x + 6)$

11) $(x - 7)(x + 7)$

12) $(x + 4)(4x - 8)$

13) $(6x - 4)(6x + 4)$

14) $(x - 7)(x + 2)$

15) $(x - 8)(x + 8)$

16) $(3x + 3)(3x - 4)$

17) $(x + 3)(x + 3)$

18) $(x + 4)(x + 6)$

Factoring Trinomials

Helpful Hints	"FOIL"	Example:
	$(x + a)(x + b) = x^2 + (b + a)x + ab$	$x^2 + 5x + 6 =$
	"Difference of Squares"	$(x + 2)(x + 3)$
	$a^2 - b^2 = (a + b)(a - b)$	
	$a^2 + 2ab + b^2 = (a + b)(a + b)$	
	$a^2 - 2ab + b^2 = (a - b)(a - b)$	
	"Reverse FOIL"	
	$x^2 + (b + a)x + ab = (x + a)(x + b)$	

✎ *Factor each trinomial.*

1) $x^2 - 7x + 12$

2) $x^2 + 5x - 14$

3) $x^2 - 11x - 42$

4) $6x^2 + x - 12$

5) $x^2 - 17x + 30$

6) $x^2 + 8x + 15$

7) $3x^2 + 11x - 4$

8) $x^2 - 6x - 27$

9) $10x^2 + 33x - 7$

10) $x^2 + 24x + 144$

11) $49x^2 + 28xy + 4y^2$

12) $16x^2 - 40x + 25$

13) $x^2 - 10x + 25$

14) $25x^2 - 20x + 4$

15) $x^3 + 6x^2y^2 + 9xy^3$

16) $9x^2 + 24x + 16$

17) $x^2 - 8x + 16$

18) $x^2 + 121 + 22x$

Operations with Polynomials

Helpful	– When multiplying a monomial by a polynomial, use the distributive property.	**Example:**
Hints	$a \times (b + c) = a \times b + a \times c$	$5(6x - 1) =$
		$30x - 5$

✎ *Find each product.*

1) $3x^2(6x - 5)$

2) $5x^2(7x - 2)$

3) $-3(8x - 3)$

4) $6x^3(-3x + 4)$

5) $9(6x + 2)$

6) $8(3x + 7)$

7) $5(6x - 1)$

8) $-7x^4(2x - 4)$

9) $8(x^2 + 2x - 3)$

10) $4(4x^2 - 2x + 1)$

11) $2(3x^2 + 2x - 2)$

12) $8x(5x^2 + 3x + 8)$

13) $(9x + 1)(3x - 1)$

14) $(4x + 5)(6x - 5)$

15) $(7x + 3)(5x - 6)$

16) $(3x - 4)(3x + 8)$

Answers of Worksheets – Chapter 9

Classifying Polynomials

1) Linear monomial
2) Quartic monomial
3) Linear binomial
4) Constant monomial
5) Linear binomial
6) Cubic binomial
7) Quantic monomial
8) Linear binomial
9) Quadratic binomial
10) Seventh degree binomial
11) Quartic polynomial with four terms
12) Quartic polynomial with four terms
13) Sixth degree trinomial
14) Quadratic trinomial
15) Sixth degree binomial
16) Seventh degree polynomial with four terms
17) Sixth degree trinomial
18) Quartic trinomial

Writing Polynomials in Standard Form

1) $-5x^3 + 3x^2$
2) $4x^3$
3) $-6x^3 + 2x^2 + x$
4) $2x$
5) $9x^4 - 7x + 12$
6) $-2x^3 + 5x^2 + 13x$
7) -3
8) $3x^2 + 10x - 8$
9) $x^2 + 3x - 10$
10) $-2x^2 - x + 12$
11) $9x^5 - x^3$
12) $-6x^3 + 6x^2 + 15x$
13) $11x^6 + 22x^4$
14) $x^2 + 9x + 18$
15) $x^2 + 8x + 16$
16) $24x^2 - 5x - 14$
17) $15x^3 + 10x^2 + 5x$
18) $42x^4 - 7x^2 + 21x$

Simplifying Polynomials

1) $-7x^3 - x^2 + 14$
2) $-x^3 + 8x^2$
3) $3x^6 - 162$
4) $-6x^3 + 24x^2 + 17$
5) $-12x^3 - x^2 + 33$
6) $3x^3 + 2x^2 - 12x$

7) $9x^2 - 36x + 32$

8) $144x^2 + 48xy + 4y^2$

9) $12x^2 + 4x + 2$

10) $6x - 1$

11) $3x^3 - 1$

12) $x^2 - 8x + 15$

13) $9x^2 - 64$

14) $16x^2 - 8x + 5$

Adding and Subtracting Polynomials

1) $4x^3$

2) $6x^3 - 2$

3) $4x^2 - 5$

4) $-x^2 + 2x$

5) $4x$

6) $6x^4 - 8x$

7) $-12x^3 + 6x$

8) $5x^3 - 13x^2$

9) $-4x^3 + 11x^2 - 6$

10) $2x^4 + 9x^3$

11) $33x^5 - 4x^4 + 16x^3$

12) $5x^5 + 23x^2 - 11x$

13) $12x^5 + 13x^4 - 3x^2 + 8$

14) $3x^5 + 10x^4 - 3x^3 + x^2 - 11$

Multiplying Monomials

1) $8xy^2z^3$

2) $4x^3y^2$

3) $-8p^5q^4$

4) $8s^5t^7$

5) $-36p^7$

6) $-24p^3q^5r^4$

7) $96a^{10}b$

8) $-21u^6v^5$

9) $-8u^4$

10) $-18x^3y^3$

11) $-12y^4z^4$

12) $10a^3b^2c^4$

Multiplying and Dividing Monomials

1) $28x^7y^{10}$

2) $45x^{13}$

3) $84x^{11}y^{21}$

4) $8x^6y^2$

5) $19x^9y^5$

6) $5y$

7) $-5x^{11}y^4$

8) $-8x^5y^3$

Multiplying a Polynomial and a Monomial

1) $15x - 30y$
2) $18x^2 + 36xy$
3) $56x^2 - 32x$
4) $36x^2 + 108x$
5) $22x^2 - 121xy$
6) $12x^2 - 12xy$
7) $6x^3 - 9x^2 + 24x$
8) $52x^2 + 104xy$

9) $40x^2 - 160x - 100$
10) $9x^2 - 6x$
11) $18x^5 - 12x^4 + 12x^3$
12) $24x^4 - 40x^3y + 56y^2x^2$
13) $6x^4 - 10x^3 + 24x^2$
14) $4x^5 + 10x^4 - 8x^3$
15) $30x^3 - 25x^2y + 10xy^2$
16) $9x^2 + 9xy - 72y^2$

Multiplying Binomials

1) $12x^2 - 2x - 4$
2) $2x^2 + 9x - 35$
3) $x^2 + 10x + 16$
4) $x^4 - 4$
5) $x^2 + 2x - 8$
6) $2x^2 - 8x - 64$
7) $15x^2 + 3x - 12$
8) $x^2 - 13x + 42$
9) $24x^2 + 90x + 81$

10) $10x^2 - 18x - 36$
11) $x^2 - 49$
12) $4x^2 + 8x - 32$
13) $36x^2 - 16$
14) $x^2 - 5x - 14$
15) $x^2 - 64$
16) $9x^2 - 3x - 12$
17) $x^2 + 6x + 9$
18) $x^2 + 10x + 24$

Factoring Trinomials

1) $(x - 3)(x - 4)$
2) $(x - 2)(x + 7)$
3) $(x + 3)(x - 14)$
4) $(2x + 3)(3x - 4)$
5) $(x - 15)(x - 2)$
6) $(x + 3)(x + 5)$
7) $(3x - 1)(x + 4)$
8) $(x - 9)(x + 3)$
9) $(5x - 1)(2x + 7)$

10) $(x + 12)(x + 12)$
11) $(7x + 2y)(7x + 2y)$
12) $(4x - 5)(4x - 5)$
13) $(x - 5)(x - 5)$
14) $(5x - 2)(5x - 2)$
15) $x(x^2 + 6xy^2 + 9y^3)$
16) $(3x + 4)(3x + 4)$
17) $(x - 4)(x - 4)$
18) $(x + 11)(x + 11)$

Operations with Polynomials

1) $18x^3 - 15x^2$

2) $35x^3 - 10x^2$

3) $-24x + 9$

4) $-18x^4 + 24x^3$

5) $54x + 18$

6) $24x + 56$

7) $30x - 5$

8) $-14x^5 + 28x^4$

9) $8x^2 + 16x - 24$

10) $16x^2 - 8x + 4$

11) $6x^2 + 4x - 4$

12) $40x^3 + 24x^2 + 64x$

13) $27x^2 - 6x - 1$

14) $24x^2 + 10x - 25$

15) $35x^2 - 27x - 18$

16) $9x^2 + 12x - 32$

Chapter 10: Quadratic and System of Equations

Math Topics that you'll learn today:

- ✓ Solve a Quadratic Equation

- ✓ Solving Systems of Equations by Substitution

- ✓ Solving Systems of Equations by Elimination

- ✓ Systems of Equations Word Problems

Mathematics is the door and key to the sciences. — Roger Bacon

Solve a Quadratic Equation

Helpful **Hints**	Write the equation in the form of $ax^2 + bx + c = 0$ Factorize the quadratic. Use quadratic formula if you couldn't factorize the quadratic. **Quadratic formula** $$x = \frac{-b \pm \sqrt{b^2 - 4ac}}{2a}$$	**Example:** $x^2 + 5x + 6 = 0$ $(x + 3)(x + 2) = 0$ $(x + 3) = 0$ $x = -3$ $x + 2 = 0$ $x = -2$

✎ *Solve each equation.*

1) $(x + 2)(x - 4) = 0$

2) $(x + 5)(x + 8) = 0$

3) $(3x + 2)(x + 3) = 0$

4) $(4x + 7)(2x + 5) = 0$

5) $x^2 - 11x + 19 = -5$

6) $x^2 + 7x + 18 = 8$

7) $x^2 - 10x + 22 = -2$

8) $x^2 + 3x - 12 = 6$

9) $18x^2 + 45x - 27 = 0$

10) $90x^2 - 84x = -18$

11) $x^2 + 8x = -15$

Solving Systems of Equations by Substitution

Helpful Hints	Consider the system of equations $x - y = 1, -2x + y = 6$ Substitute x = 1 − y in the second equation $-2(1 - y) + y = 5 \qquad y = 2$ Substitute $y = 2$ in $x = 1 + y$ $x = 1 + 2 = 3$	Example: $-2x - 2y = -13$ $-4x + 2y = 10$ (0.5, 6)

Solve each system of equation by substitution.

1) $-2x + 2y = 4$

$-2x + y = 3$

4) $2y = -6x + 10$

$10x - 8y = -6$

2) $-10x + 2y = -6$

$6x - 16y = 48$

5) $3x - 9y = -3$

$3y = 3x - 3$

3) $y = -8$

$16x - 12y = 72$

6) $-4x + 12y = 12$

$-14x + 16y = -10$

Solving Systems of Equations by Elimination

Helpful *Hints*	-	The elimination method for solving systems of linear equations uses the addition property of equality. You can add the same value to each side of an equation.	**Example:** $x + 2y = 6$ $+ -x + y = 3$ $3y = 9$ $y = 3$ $x + 6 = 6$ $x = 0$

Solve each system of equation by elimination.

1) $10x - 9y = -12$

  $-5x + 3y = 6$

2) $-3x - 4y = 5$

  $x - 2y = 5$

3) $5x - 14y = 22$

  $-6x + 7y = 3$

4) $10x - 14y = -4$

  $-10x - 20y = -30$

5) $32x + 14y = 52$

  $16x - 4y = -40$

6) $2x - 8y = -6$

  $8x + 2y = 10$

7) $-4x + 4y = -4$

  $4x + 2y = 10$

8) $4x + 6y = 10$

  $8x + 12y = -20$

Systems of Equations Word Problems

Helpful	Define your variables, Write two equations, and use one of the methods for solving systems of equations to solve.
Hints	

Example:

The difference of two numbers is 6. Their sum is 14. Find the numbers.

$x + y = 6$

$x + y = 14$ $(10, 4)$

1) A farmhouse shelters 10 animals, some are pigs and some are ducks. Altogether there are 36 legs. How many of each animal are there?

2) A class 0f 195 students went on a field trip. They took vehicles, some cars and some buses. Find the number of cars and the number of buses they took if each car holds 5 students and each bus hold 45 students.

3) The sum of the digits of a certain two–digit number is 7. Reversing its increasing the number by 9. What is the number?

4) A boat traveled 336 miles downstream and back. The trip downstream took 12 hours. The trip back took 14 hours. What is the speed of the boat in still water? What is the speed of the current?

Answers of Worksheets – Chapter 10

Solving Quadratic Equations

1) $x = -2, x = 4$

2) $x = -5, x = -8$

3) $x = -\frac{2}{3}, x = -3$

4) $x = -\frac{7}{4}, x = -\frac{5}{2}$

5) $x = 8, x = 3$

6) $x = -5, x = -2$

7) $x = 6, x = 4$

8) $x = -6, x = 3$

9) $x = \frac{1}{2}, x = -3$

10) $x = \frac{3}{5}, x = \frac{1}{3}$

11) $x = -5, x = -3$

Solving Systems of Equations by Substitution

1) (4, 9)

2) (−1, 1)

3) (0, −3)

4) (−24, −8)

5) (1, 2)

6) (4, 3)

7) (3, 2)

8) (−5, 1)

Solving Systems of Equations by Elimination

1) (15, 27)

2) (1, −2)

3) (−4, −3)

4) (1, 1)

5) (−1, 6)

6) (1, 1)

7) (2, 1)

8) No solution

9) (3, 4)

10) (4, 2)

Systems of Equations Word Problems

1) (2, 8)

2) (3, 4)

3) (10, 4)

4) 34

5) boat: 26 mph, current: 2 mph

Chapter 11: Quadratic Functions

Math Topics that you'll learn today:

- ✓ Graphing quadratic functions in standard form

- ✓ Graphing quadratic functions in vertex form

- ✓ Solving quadratic equations

- ✓ Use the quadratic formula and the discriminant

- ✓ Operations with complex numbers

- ✓ Solve quadratic inequalities

It's fine to work on any problem, so long as it generates interesting mathematics along the way – even if you don't solve it at the end of the day." – Andrew Wiles

Graphing quadratic functions in standard form

Helpful

Hints

- Quadratic functions in standard form

  $$ax^2 + bx + c = 0$$

Sketch the graph of each function.

1) $y = 2x^2$

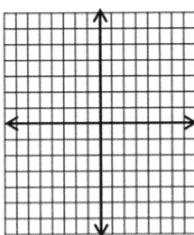

2) $y = 4x^2$

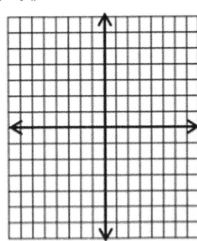

3) $y = -4x^2$

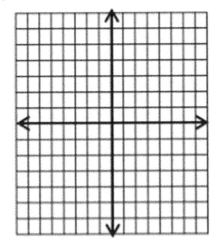

4) $y = 2x^2$

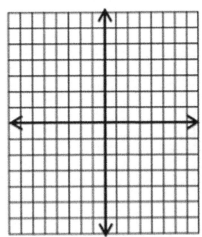

Graphing quadratic functions in vertex form

> *Helpful*
>
> *Hints*
>
> - Quadratic functions in standard form
>
> $$y = a\,(x - h)^2 + k$$

Sketch the graph of each function. Identify the vertex and axis of symmetry.

1) $= 3(+ 1)^2 + 2$

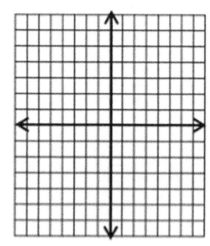

2) $= -(- 2)^2 - 4$

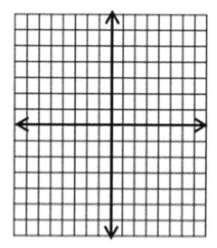

3) $- 2(2)^2 + 8$

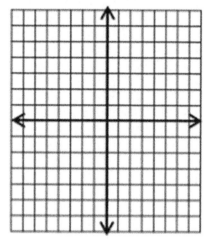

4) $= {}^2 - 8 + 19$

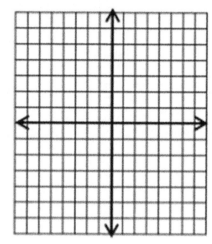

Solving quadratic equations by factoring

Helpful	-	For $ax^2 + bx + c = 0$, the values of x which are the solutions of the equation are given by:	**Example:**
Hints		$$x = \frac{-b \pm \sqrt{b^2 - 4ac}}{2a}$$	

Solve each equation by factoring.

1) $x^2 + x - 20 = 2x$

2) $x^2 + 8x = -15$

3) $7x^2 - 14x = -7$

4) $6x^2 - 18x - 18 = 6$

5) $2x^2 + 6x - 24 = 12$

6) $2x^2 - 22x + 38 = -10$

7) $(2x + 5)(4x + 3) = 0$

8) $(x + 2)(x - 7) = 0$

9) $(x + 3)(x + 5) = 0$

10) $(5x + 7)(x + 4) = 0$

11) $-4x^2 - 8x - 3 = -3 - 5x^2$

12) $10x^2 = 27x - 18$

13) $7x^2 - 6x + 3 = 3$

14) $x^2 = 2x$

15) $2x^2 - 14 = -3x$

16) $10x^2 - 26x = -12$

17) $15x^2 + 80 = -80x$

18) $x^2 + 15x = -56$

Use the quadratic formula and the discriminant

Helpful — The discriminant color, is the part of the quadratic formula under the square root.

Hints

$$x = \frac{-b \pm \sqrt{b^2 - 4a}}{2a}$$

Find the value of the discriminant of each quadratic equation.

1) $2x^2 + 5x - 4 = 0$

2) $x^2 + 5x + 2 = 0$

3) $5x^2 + x - 2 = 0$

4) $-4x^2 - 4x + 5 = 0$

5) $-2x^2 - x - 1 = 0$

6) $6x^2 - 2x - 3 = 0$

7) $x\,(x - 1)$

8) $8x^2 - 9x = 0$

9) $3x^2 - 5x + 1 = 0$

10) $5x^2 + 6x + 4 = 0$

Find the discriminant of each quadratic equation then state the number of real and imaginary solution.

11) $8x^2 - 6x + 3 = 5x^2$

12) $-4x^2 - 4x = 6$

13) $-x^2 - 9 = 6x$

14) $-9x^2 = -8x + 8$

15) $4x^2 = 8x - 4$

16) $9x^2 + 6x + 6 = 5$

17) $9x^2 - 3x - 8 = -10$

18) $-2x^2 - 8x - 14 = -6$

Operations with complex numbers

Helpful	- **Addition**
	$(a_1 + b_1i) + (a_2 + b_2i) = (a_1 + a_2) + (b_1 + b_2)i$
Hints	- **Subtraction**
	$(a_1 + b_1i) - (a_2 + b_2i) = (a_1 - a_2) + (b_1 - b_2)i$
	- **Multiplication**
	$(a_1 + b_1i) \cdot (a_2 + b_2i) = (a_1a_2 - b_1b_2) + (a_1b_2 + a_2b_1)i$

Simplify.

1) $-3i \cdot 6i$

2) $8i \cdot i \cdot -2i$

3) $(5 - 3i)(3 + i)$

4) $8i \cdot 2i (-5 - 3i)$

5) $(-2 - i)(4 + i)$

6) $(8 - 4i)(-9 + 5i)$

7) $(-5 + 3i)(-7 - 9i)$

8) $(8 - 6i)(-4 - 4i)$

9) $(5i)^3$

10) $6i + 8i \cdot i$

11) $-8(5 - 5i)$

12) $(8 - 3i)^2$

13) $6 + 4i - 8i - 8$

14) $-5i \cdot 2i - 5(-5 + 3i)$

15) $-4i(5 - 9i)(-2 - 8i)$

16) $8(-4 + 7i)(-4 + 5i)$

17) $(1 - 7i)^2$

18) $(2 - 4i)(-6 + 4i)$

Solve quadratic inequalities

Helpful *Hints*	- A quadratic inequality is one that can be written in one of the following standard forms: $ax^2 + bx + c > 0$ $ax^2 + bx + c < 0$ $ax^2 + bx + c \geq 0$ $ax^2 + bx + c \leq 0$	**Example:**

Solve each quadratic inequality.

1) $-x^2 - 5x + 6 > 0$

2) $x^2 - 5x - 6 < 0$

3) $x^2 + 4x - 5 > 0$

4) $x^2 - 2x - 3 \geq 0$

5) $x^2 - 1 < 0$

6) $17x^2 + 15x - 2 \geq 0$

7) $4x^2 + 20x - 11 < 0$

8) $12x^2 + 10x - 12 > 0$

9) $18x^2 + 23x + 5 \leq 0$

10) $-9x^2 + 29x - 6 \geq 0$

11) $-8x^2 + 6x - 1 \leq 0$

12) $5x^2 - 15x + 10 < 0$

13) $3x^2 - 5x \geq 4x^2 + 6$

14) $x^2 > 5x + 6$

15) $3x^2 + 7x \leq 5x^2 + 3x - 6$

16) $4x^2 - 12 > 3x^2 + x$

17) $3x^2 - 5x \geq 4x^2 + 6$

18) $2x^2 + 2x - 8 > x^2$

Answers of Worksheets – Chapter 11

Graphing quadratic functions in standard form

1)

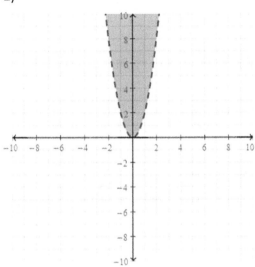

2)

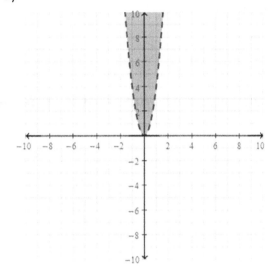

3)

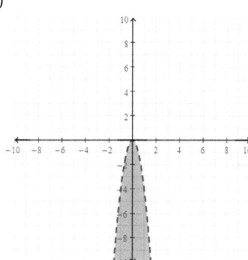

4)

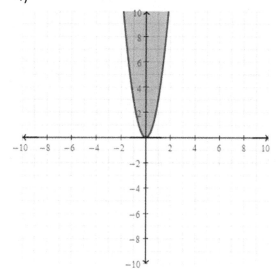

Graphing quadratic functions in vertex form

1)

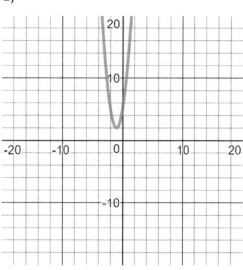

2)

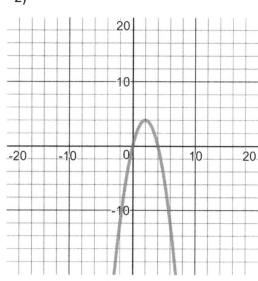

3)

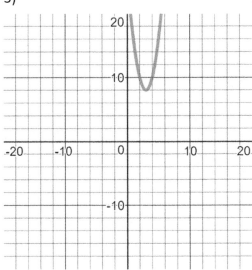

4)

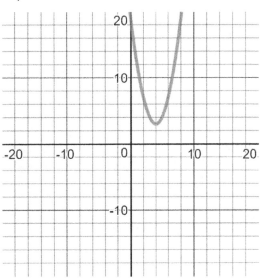

Solving quadratic equations by factoring

1) $\{5, -4\}$

2) $\{-5, -3\}$

3) $\{1\}$

4) $\{4, -1\}$

5) $\{3, -6\}$

6) $\{3, 8\}$

7) $\{-\frac{5}{2}, -\frac{3}{4}\}$

8) $\{-2, 7\}$

9) $\{-3, -5\}$

10) $\{-\frac{7}{5}, -4\}$

11) $\{8, 0\}$

12) $\{\frac{6}{5}, \frac{3}{2}\}$

13) $\{\frac{6}{7}, 0\}$

14) $\{2, 0\}$

15) $\{-\frac{7}{2}, 2\}$

16) $\{\frac{3}{5}, 2\}$

17) $\{-\frac{4}{3}, -4\}$

18) $\{-8, -7\}$

Use the quadratic formula and the discriminant

1) 57

2) 17

3) 41

4) 96

5) −7

6) 76

7) 21

8) 81

9) 13

10) −44

11) 0, one real solution

12) −80, two imaginary solutions

13) 0, one real solution

14) −224, two imaginary solutions

15) 0, one real solution

16) 0, one real solution

17) −63, two imaginary solutions

18) 0, one real solution

Operations with complex numbers

1) 18

2) 18i

3) 18 − 4i

4) 80 + 48i

5) −7 − 6i

6) −52 + 76i

7) 62 + 24i

8) −56 − 8i

9) −125i

10) − 8 + 6i

11) − 40 + 40i

12) 55 − 48i

13) − 2 + 4i

14) 35 − 15i

15) − 88 + 328i

16) −152 − 384i

17) −48 − 14i

18) 4 + 32i

Solve quadratic inequalities

1) $-6 < x < 1$

2) $-1 < x < 6$

3) $x < -5$ or $x > 1$

4) $x \leq -1$ or $x \geq 3$

5) $-1 < x < 1$

6) $x \leq -1$ or $x \geq \frac{2}{17}$

7) $-\frac{11}{2} < x < \frac{1}{2}$

8) $x < -\frac{3}{2}$ or $x > \frac{2}{3}$

9) $-1 \leq x \leq -\frac{5}{18}$

10) $\frac{2}{9} \leq x \leq 3$

11) $x \leq \frac{1}{4}$ or $x \geq \frac{1}{2}$

12) $1 < x < 2$

13) $-3 \leq x \leq -2$

14) $x < -1$ or $x > 6$

15) $x \leq -1$ or $x \geq 3$

16) $x < -3$ or $x > 4$

17) $-3 \leq x \leq -2$

18) $x < -4$ or $x > 2$

Chapter 12: complex numbers

Math Topics that you'll learn today:

✓ Adding and subtracting complex numbers

✓ Multiplying and dividing complex numbers

✓ Graphing complex numbers

✓ Rationalizing imaginary denominators

Mathematics is a hard thing to love. It has the unfortunate habit, like a rude dog, of turning its most unfavorable side towards you when you first make contact with it. — David Whiteland

Adding and subtracting complex numbers

Helpful	**Adding:**	**Example:**

$$(a + bi) + (c + di) = (a + c) + (b + d)i$$

$$-5 + (2 - 4i) = -3 - 4i$$

Hints **Subtracting:**

$$(2 - 5i) + (4 - 6i) =$$

$$(a + bi) - (c + di) = (a - c) + (b - d)i$$

$$6 - 11i$$

Simplify.

1) $-8 + (2i) + (-8 + 6i)$

2) $12 - (5i) + (4 - 14i)$

3) $-2 + (-8 - 7i) - 9$

4) $(-18 - 3i) + (11 + 5i)$

5) $(3 + 5i) + (8 + 3i)$

6) $(8 - 3i) + (4 + i)$

7) $3 + (2 - 4i)$

8) $(10 + 9i) + (6 + 8i)$

9) $(-5i) - (-5 + 2i)$

10) $(-14 + i) - (-12 - 11i)$

11) $(-12i) + (2 - 6i) + 10$

12) $(-11 - 9i) - (-9 - 3i)$

13) $(13i) - (17 + 3i)$

14) $(-3 + 6i) - (-9 - i)$

15) $(-5 + 15i) - (-3 + 3i)$

16) $(-12i) + (2 - 6i) + 10$

Multiplying and dividing complex numbers

Helpful Hints

Multiplying:

$$(a + bi) + (c + di) = (ac - bd) + (ad + bc)i$$

Dividing:

$$\frac{a+bi}{c+di} = \frac{a+bi}{c+di} \cdot \frac{c-di}{c-di} = \frac{ac+}{c^2+d^2} + \frac{bc+ad}{c^2+d^2}i$$

Simplify.

1) $(4i)(-i)(2-5i)$

2) $(2-8i)(3-5i)$

3) $(-5+9i)(3+5i)$

4) $(7+3i)(7+8i)$

5) $(5+4i)^2$

6) $2(3i) - (5i)(-8+5i)$

7) $\dfrac{2+4i}{14+4i}$

8) $\dfrac{4-3i}{-4i}$

9) $\dfrac{5+6i}{-1+8i}$

10) $\dfrac{-8-i}{-4-6i}$

11) $\dfrac{5+9i}{i}$

12) $\dfrac{12i}{-9+3i}$

13) $\dfrac{5}{-10i}$

14) $\dfrac{-3-10}{5i}$

15) $\dfrac{9i}{3-i}$

16) $\dfrac{-1+5i}{-8-7i}$

17) $\dfrac{-2-9i}{-2+7i}$

18) $\dfrac{4+i}{2-5i}$

Graphing complex numbers

Helpful	- Complex numbers can be plotted on the complex coordinate plane.
	- The horizontal line is Real axis and the vertical line is Imaginary axis.
Hints	- Complex numbers are written in the form of: $A + Bi$, where A is real number and B is number of units up or down.
	For example: The point 3 + 4i, is located 3 units to the right of origin and 4 units up.

Identify each complex number graphed.

1)

2)

3)

4)

Rationalizing imaginary denominators

Helpful *Hints*	Step 1: Find the conjugate (it's the denominator with different sign between the two terms.
	Step 2: Multiply numerator and denominator by the conjugate.
	Step 3: Simplify if needed.
	Example: $\dfrac{5i}{2-3i} = \dfrac{5i(2+3i)}{(2-3i)(2+3i)} = \dfrac{10i+1^{2}}{4-9i^2} = \dfrac{-15+1}{13}$

Simplify.

1) $\dfrac{10-10}{-5i}$

2) $\dfrac{4-9i}{-6i}$

3) $\dfrac{6+8i}{9i}$

4) $\dfrac{8i}{-1+3i}$

5) $\dfrac{5i}{-2-6i}$

6) $\dfrac{-10-5i}{-6+6i}$

7) $\dfrac{-5-9i}{9+8i}$

8) $\dfrac{-5-3i}{7-10i}$

9) $\dfrac{-1+i}{-5i}$

10) $\dfrac{-6-i}{i}$

11) $\dfrac{a}{ib}$

12) $\dfrac{-4-i}{9+5i}$

13) $\dfrac{-3+i}{-2i}$

14) $\dfrac{-5}{-i}$

15) $\dfrac{-6-i}{-1+6i}$

16) $\dfrac{-9-3i}{-3+3i}$

17) $\dfrac{6}{-4i}$

18) $\dfrac{8i}{-1+3i}$

Answers of Worksheets – Chapter 12

Adding and subtracting complex numbers

1) $-16 + 8i$

2) $16 - 19i$

3) $-19 - 7i$

4) $-7 + 2i$

5) $11 + 8i$

6) $12 - 2i$

7) $5 - 4i$

8) $16 + 17i$

9) $5 - 7i$

10) $-2 + 12i$

11) $12 - 18i$

12) $-2 - 6i$

13) $-17 + 10i$

14) $6 + 7i$

15) $-2 + 12i$

16) $12 - 18i$

Multiplying and dividing complex numbers

1) $8 - 20i$

2) $-34 - 34i$

3) $-60 + 2i$

4) $25 + 77i$

5) $9 + 40i$

6) $25 + 46i$

7) $\frac{11+12}{53}$

8) $\frac{3}{4} + i$

9) $\frac{19}{26} - \frac{11}{13}i$

10) $\frac{2-6i}{5}$

11) $-5i + 9$

12) $\frac{-3i+1}{6}$

13) $\frac{i}{2}$

14) $\frac{3i-10}{5}$

15) $\frac{27i-9}{10}$

16) $-\frac{27}{113} - \frac{47i}{113}$

17) $-\frac{59}{53} + \frac{32}{53}$

18) $\frac{3}{29} + \frac{22i}{29}$

Graphing complex numbers

1) $1 - 4i$

2) $1 + 3i$

3) $2 + 4i$

4) $4 + 2i$

Rationalizing imaginary denominators

1) $2i + 2$

2) $\dfrac{4 + 9i}{6}$

3) $\dfrac{6+8i}{9}$

4) $\dfrac{-4i+1}{5}$

5) $\dfrac{-i-3}{4}$

6) $\dfrac{5+15i}{12}$

7) $\dfrac{-117-41i}{145}$

8) $\dfrac{-5-71i}{149}$

9) $\dfrac{-i-1}{5}$

10) $6i - 1$

11) $-\dfrac{ia}{b}$

12) $\dfrac{-41+1}{106}$

13) $\dfrac{-1-3i}{2}$

14) $-5i$

15) $0 + 1i$

16) $-3 + 3i$

17) $\dfrac{3i}{2}$

18) $\dfrac{-4i+1}{5}$

Chapter 13: Exponents and Radicals

Math Topics that you'll learn today:

- ✓ Multiplication Property of Exponents
- ✓ Division Property of Exponents
- ✓ Powers of Products and Quotients
- ✓ Zero and Negative Exponents
- ✓ Negative Exponents and Negative Bases
- ✓ Writing Scientific Notation
- ✓ Square Roots

Mathematics is no more computation than typing is literature.

– John Allen Paulos

Multiplication Property of Exponents

Helpful	Exponents rules	Example:
Hints	$x^a \cdot x^b = x^{a+b}$ $\qquad$ $x^a/x^b = x^{a-b}$	$(x^2y)^3 = x^6y^3$
	$1/x^b = x^{-b}$ $\qquad$ $(x^a)^b = x^{a.b}$	
	$(xy)^a = x^a \cdot y^a$	

✎ *Simplify.*

1) $4^2 \cdot 4^2$

2) $2 \cdot 2^2 \cdot 2^2$

3) $3^2 \cdot 3^2$

4) $3x^3 \cdot x$

5) $12x^4 \cdot 3x$

6) $6x \cdot 2x^2$

7) $5x^4 \cdot 5x^4$

8) $6x^2 \cdot 6x^3y^4$

9) $7x^2y^5 \cdot 9xy^3$

10) $7xy^4 \cdot 4x^3y^3$

11) $(2x^2)^2$

12) $3x^5y^3 \cdot 8x^2y^3$

13) $7x^3 \cdot 10y^3x^5 \cdot 8yx^3$

14) $(x^4)^3$

15) $(2x^2)^4$

16) $(x^2)^3$

17) $(6x)^2$

18) $3x^4y^5 \cdot 7x^2y^3$

Division Property of Exponents

Helpful	$\frac{x^a}{x^b} = x^{a-b} \, , \, x \neq 0$	Example:
Hints		$\frac{x^{12}}{x^5} = x^7$

✍ *Simplify.*

1) $\frac{5^5}{5}$

2) $\frac{3}{3^5}$

3) $\frac{2^2}{2^3}$

4) $\frac{2^4}{2^2}$

5) $\frac{x}{x^3}$

6) $\frac{3x^3}{9x^4}$

7) $\frac{2x^{-5}}{9x^{-2}}$

8) $\frac{21^8}{7x^3}$

9) $\frac{7x^6}{4x^7}$

10) $\frac{6x^2}{4x^3}$

11) $\frac{5x}{10x^3}$

12) $\frac{3x^3}{2x^5}$

13) $\frac{12^3}{14^6}$

14) $\frac{12^3}{9y^8}$

15) $\frac{25xy^4}{5x^6y^2}$

16) $\frac{2x^4}{7x}$

17) $\frac{16x^2y^8}{4x^3}$

18) $\frac{12x^4}{15x^7y^9}$

19) $\frac{12yx^4}{10y^8}$

20) $\frac{16x^4y}{9x^8y^2}$

21) $\frac{5x^8}{20x^8}$

Powers of Products and Quotients

Helpful	For any nonzero numbers a and b and any integer x, $(ab)^x = a^x \cdot b^x$.	**Example:**
Hints		$(2x^2 \cdot y^3)^2 =$ $4x^2 \cdot y^6$

✎*Simplify.*

1) $(2x^3)^4$

2) $(4xy^4)^2$

3) $(5x^4)^2$

4) $(11x^5)^2$

5) $(4x^2y^4)^4$

6) $(2x^4y^4)^3$

7) $(3x^2y^2)^2$

8) $(3x^4y^3)^4$

9) $(2x^6y^8)^2$

10) $(12x \; 3x)^3$

11) $(2x^9 \; x^6)^3$

12) $(5x^{10}y^3)^3$

13) $(4x^3 \; x^2)^2$

14) $(3x^3 \; 5x)^2$

15) $(10x^{11}y^3)^2$

16) $(9x^7 \; y^5)^2$

17) $(4x^4y^6)^5$

18) $(4x^4)^2$

19) $(3x \; 4y^3)^2$

20) $(9x^2y)^3$

21) $(12x^2y^5)^2$

Zero and Negative Exponents

Helpful *Hints*	A negative exponent simply means that the base is on the wrong side of the fraction line, so you need to flip the base to the other side. For instance, "x^{-2}" (pronounced as "ecks to the minus two") just means "x^2" but underneath, as in $\frac{1}{x^2}$	**Example:** $5^{-2} = \frac{1}{25}$

✎ *Evaluate the following expressions.*

1) 8^{-2}

2) 2^{-4}

3) 10^{-2}

4) 5^{-3}

5) 22^{-1}

6) 9^{-1}

7) 3^{-2}

8) 4^{-2}

9) 5^{-2}

10) 35^{-1}

11) 6^{-3}

12) 0^{15}

13) 10^{-9}

14) 3^{-4}

15) 5^{-2}

16) 2^{-3}

17) 3^{-3}

18) 8^{-1}

19) 7^{-3}

20) 6^{-2}

21) $(\frac{2}{3})^{-2}$

22) $(\frac{1}{5})^{-3}$

23) $(\frac{1}{2})^{-8}$

24) $(\frac{2}{5})^{-3}$

Negative Exponents and Negative Bases

Helpful	– Make the power positive. A negative exponent is the reciprocal of that number with a positive exponent.	**Example:**
Hints	– The parenthesis is important!	$2x^{-3} = \dfrac{2}{x^3}$

-5^{-2} is not the same as $(-5)^{-2}$

$-5^{-2} = -\dfrac{1}{5^2}$ and $(-5)^{-2} = +\dfrac{1}{5^2}$

✎ *Simplify.*

1) -6^{-1}

2) $-4x^{-3}$

3) $-\dfrac{5x}{x^{-3}}$

4) $-\dfrac{a^{-3}}{b^{-2}}$

5) $-\dfrac{5}{x^{-3}}$

6) $\dfrac{7b}{-9c^{-4}}$

7) $-\dfrac{5n^{-2}}{10^{-3}}$

8) $\dfrac{4a^{-2}}{-3c^{-2}}$

9) $-12x^2y^{-3}$

10) $\left(-\dfrac{1}{3}\right)^{-2}$

11) $\left(-\dfrac{3}{4}\right)^{-2}$

12) $\left(\dfrac{3a}{2c}\right)^{-2}$

13) $\left(-\dfrac{5x}{3yz}\right)^{-3}$

14) $-\dfrac{2x}{a^{-4}}$

Writing Scientific Notation

Helpful	– It is used to write very big or very small numbers in decimal form. – In scientific notation all numbers are written in the form of: $$m \times 10^n$$

Hints

Decimal notation	Scientific notation
5	5×10^0
−25,000	$−2.5 \times 10^4$
0.5	5×10^{-1}
2,122.456	$2,122456 \times 10^3$

✍ *Write each number in scientific notation.*

1) 91×10^3

2) 60

3) 2000000

4) 0.0000006

5) 354000

6) 0.000325

7) 2.5

8) 0.00023

9) 56000000

10) 2000000

11) 78000000

12) 0.0000022

13) 0.00012

14) 0.004

15) 78

16) 1600

17) 1450

18) 130000

19) 60

20) 0.113

21) 0.02

Square Roots

Helpful	− A square root of x is a number r whose square is: $r^2 = x$	**Example:**
Hints	r is a square root of x.	$\sqrt{4} = 2$

✍️ *Find the value each square root.*

1) $\sqrt{1}$

2) $\sqrt{4}$

3) $\sqrt{9}$

4) $\sqrt{25}$

5) $\sqrt{16}$

6) $\sqrt{49}$

7) $\sqrt{36}$

8) $\sqrt{0}$

9) $\sqrt{64}$

10) $\sqrt{81}$

11) $\sqrt{121}$

12) $\sqrt{225}$

13) $\sqrt{144}$

14) $\sqrt{100}$

15) $\sqrt{256}$

16) $\sqrt{289}$

17) $\sqrt{324}$

18) $\sqrt{400}$

19) $\sqrt{900}$

20) $\sqrt{529}$

21) $\sqrt{90}$

Answers of Worksheets – Chapter 13

Multiplication Property of Exponents

1) 4^4
2) 2^5
3) 3^4
4) $3x^4$
5) $36x^5$
6) $12x^3$

7) $25x^8$
8) $36x^5y^4$
9) $63x^3y^8$
10) $28x^4y^7$
11) $4x^4$
12) $24x^7y^6$

13) $560x^{11}y^4$
14) x^{12}
15) $16x^8$
16) x^6
17) $36x^2$
18) $21x^6y^8$

Division Property of Exponents

1) 5^4

2) $\dfrac{1}{3^4}$

3) $\dfrac{1}{2}$

4) 2^2

5) $\dfrac{1}{x^2}$

6) $\dfrac{1}{3x}$

7) $\dfrac{2}{9x^3}$

8) $3x^5$

9) $\dfrac{7}{4x}$

10) $\dfrac{3}{2x}$

11) $\dfrac{1}{2x^2}$

12) $\dfrac{3}{2x^2}$

13) $\dfrac{6}{7x^3}$

14) $\dfrac{4x^3}{3y^8}$

15) $\dfrac{5y^2}{x^5}$

16) $\dfrac{2x^3}{7}$

17) $\dfrac{4y^8}{x}$

18) $\dfrac{4}{5x^3y^9}$

19) $\dfrac{6}{5x^4}$

20) $\dfrac{16}{9x^4y}$

21) $\dfrac{1}{4}$

Powers of Products and Quotients

1) $16x^{12}$

2) $16x^2y^8$

3) $25x^8$

4) $121x^{10}$

5) $256x^8y^{16}$

6) $8x^{12}y^{12}$

7) $9x^4y^4$

8) $81x^{16}y^{12}$

9) $4x^{12}y^{16}$

10) $46,656x^6$

11) $8x^{45}$

12) $125x^{30}y^9$

13) $16x^{10}$

14) $225x^8$

15) $100x^{22}y^6$

16) $81x^{14}y^{10}$

17) $1,024x^{20}y^{30}$

18) $16x^8$

19) $144x^2y^6$ 20) $729x^6y^3$ 21) $144x^4y^{10}$

Zero and Negative Exponents

1) $\dfrac{1}{64}$ 9) $\dfrac{1}{25}$ 17) $\dfrac{1}{27}$

2) $\dfrac{1}{16}$ 10) $\dfrac{1}{35}$ 18) $\dfrac{1}{8}$

3) $\dfrac{1}{100}$ 11) $\dfrac{1}{216}$ 19) $\dfrac{1}{343}$

4) $\dfrac{1}{125}$ 12) 0 20) $\dfrac{1}{36}$

5) $\dfrac{1}{22}$ 13) $\dfrac{1}{1000000000}$ 21) $\dfrac{9}{4}$

6) $\dfrac{1}{9}$ 14) $\dfrac{1}{81}$ 22) 125

7) $\dfrac{1}{9}$ 15) $\dfrac{1}{25}$ 23) 256

8) $\dfrac{1}{16}$ 16) $\dfrac{1}{8}$ 24) $\dfrac{125}{8}$

Negative Exponents and Negative Bases

1) $-\dfrac{1}{6}$ 6) $-\dfrac{7bc^4}{9}$ 10) 9

2) $-\dfrac{4}{x^3}$ 7) $-\dfrac{p^3}{2n^2}$ 11) $\dfrac{16}{9}$

3) $-5x^4$ 8) $-\dfrac{4ac^2}{3b^2}$ 12) $\dfrac{4c^2}{9a^2}$

4) $-\dfrac{b^2}{a^3}$ 9) $-\dfrac{12^{\ 2}}{y^3}$ 13) $-\dfrac{27y^3z^3}{125x^3}$

5) $-5x^3$ 14) $-2xa^4$

Writing Scientific Notation

1) 9.1×10^4 6) 3.25×10^{-4} 11) 7.8×10^7

2) 6×10^1 7) 2.5×10^0 12) 2.2×10^{-6}

3) 2×10^6 8) 2.3×10^{-4} 13) 1.2×10^{-4}

4) 6×10^{-7} 9) 5.6×10^7 14) 4×10^{-3}

5) 3.54×10^5 10) 2×10^6 15) 7.8×10^1

16) 1.6×10^3

17) 1.45×10^3

18) 1.3×10^5

19) 6×10^1

20) 1.13×10^{-1}

21) 2×10^{-2}

Square Roots

1) 1

2) 2

3) 3

4) 5

5) 4

6) 7

7) 6

8) 0

9) 8

10) 9

11) 11

12) 15

13) 12

14) 10

15) 16

16) 17

17) 18

18) 20

19) 30

20) 23

21) $3\sqrt{10}$

Chapter 14: Statistics

Math Topics that you'll learn today:

- ✓ Mean, Median, Mode, and Range of the Given Data
- ✓ Box and Whisker Plots
- ✓ Bar Graph
- ✓ Stem– And– Leaf Plot
- ✓ The Pie Graph or Circle Graph
- ✓ Scatter Plots

Mathematics is no more computation than typing is literature.

– John Allen Paulos

Mean, Median, Mode, and Range of the Given Data

Helpful	-	Mean: $\dfrac{\text{sum of the data}}{\text{of data entires}}$	**Example:**
	-	Mode: value in the list that appears most often	22, 16, 12, 9, 7, 6, 4, 6
Hints	-	Range: largest value – smallest value	Mean = 10.25
			Mod = 6
			Range = 18

✎*Find Mean, Median, Mode, and Range of the Given Data.*

1) 7, 2, 5, 1, 1, 2

2) 2, 2, 2, 3, 6, 3, 7, 4

3) 9, 4, 3, 1, 7, 9, 4, 6, 4

4) 8, 4, 2, 4, 3, 2, 4, 5

5) 8, 5, 7, 5, 7, 9, 8

6) 5, 1, 4, 4, 9, 2, 9, 2, 5, 1

7) 4, 1, 5, 9, 7, 7, 5, 4, 3, 5

8) 7, 5, 4, 9, 6, 7, 7, 5, 2

9) 2, 5, 5, 6, 2, 4, 7, 6, 4, 9

10) 10, 5, 2, 5, 4, 5, 8, 10

11) 5, 1, 5, 2, 2

12) 2, 3, 5, 9, 6

Box and Whisker Plots

Helpful	Box–and–whisker plots display data including quartiles.
	- IQR – interquartile range shows the difference from Q1 to Q3.
Hints	- Extreme Values are the smallest and largest values in a data set.

Example:

73, 84, 86, 95, 68, 67, 100, 94, 77, 80, 62, 79

Maximum: 100, Minimum: 62, Q_1: 70.5, Q_2: 79.5, Q_3: 90

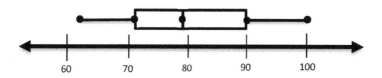

✎*Make box and whisker plots for the given data.*

11, 17, 22, 18, 23, 2, 3, 16, 21, 7, 8, 15, 5

Bar Graph

Helpful	– A bar graph is a chart that presents data with bars in different heights to match with the values of the data. The bars can be graphed horizontally or vertically.
Hints	

✍ *Graph the given information as a bar graph.*

Day	Hot dogs sold
Monday	90
Tuesday	70
Wednesday	30
Thursday	20
Friday	60

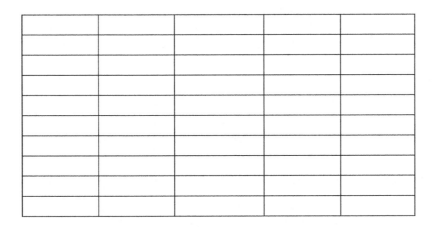

Monday   Tuesday   Wednesday   Thursday   Friday

Stem–And–Leaf Plot

Helpful	– Stem–and–leaf plots display the frequency of the values in a data set.
Hints	– We can make a frequency distribution table for the values, or we can use a stem–and–leaf plot.

Example:

56, 58, 42, 48, 66, 64, 53, 69, 45, 72

Stem	leaf
4	2 5 8
5	3 6 8
6	4 6 9
7	2

✍ *Make stem ad leaf plots for the given data.*

1) 74, 88, 97, 72, 79, 86, 95, 79, 83, 91

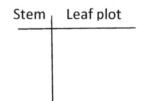

2) 37, 48, 26, 33, 49, 26, 19, 26, 48

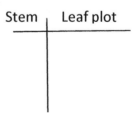

3) 58, 41, 42, 67, 54, 65, 65, 54, 69, 53

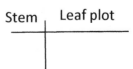

The Pie Graph or Circle Graph

Helpful	A Pie Chart is a circle chart divided into sectors, each sector represents the relative size of each value.
Hints	

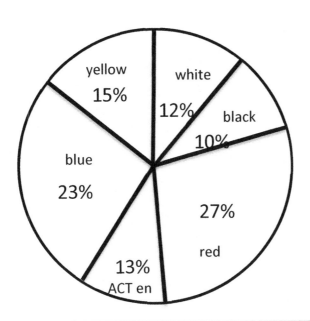

Favorite colors

1) Which color is the most?

2) What percentage of pie graph is yellow?

3) Which color is the least?

4) What percentage of pie graph is blue?

5) What percentage of pie graph is ACT en?

Scatter Plots

Helpful	A Scatter (xy) Plot shows the values with points that represent the relationship between two sets of data.
Hints	– The horizontal values are usually x and vertical data is y.

✍ *Construct a scatter plot.*

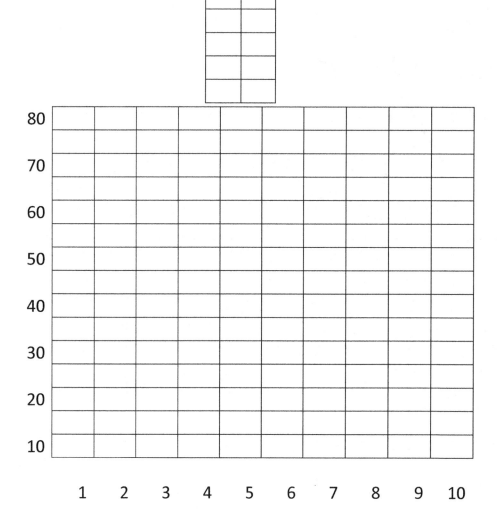

Answers of Worksheets – Chapter 14

Mean, Median, Mode, and Range of the Given Data

1) mean: 3, median: 2, mode: 1, 2, range: 6
2) mean: 3.625, median: 3, mode: 2, range: 5
3) mean: 5.22, median: 4, mode: 4, range: 8
4) mean: 4, median: 4, mode: 4, range: 6
5) mean: 7, median: 7, mode: 5, 7, 8, range: 4
6) mean: 4.2, median: 4, mode: 1,2,4,5,9, range: 8
7) mean: 5, median: 5, mode: 5, range: 8
8) mean: 5.78, median: 6, mode: 7, range: 7
9) mean: 5, median: 5, mode: 2, 4, 5, 6, range: 7
10) mean: 6.125, median: 5, mode: 5, range: 8
11) mean: 3, median: 2, mode: 2, 5, range: 4
12) mean: 5, median: 5, mode: none, range: 7

Box and Whisker Plots

11, 17, 22, 18, 23, 2, 3, 16, 21, 7, 8, 15, 5

Maximum: 23, Minimum: 2, Q_1: 2, Q_2: 12.5, Q_3: 19.5

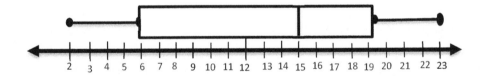

Bar Graph

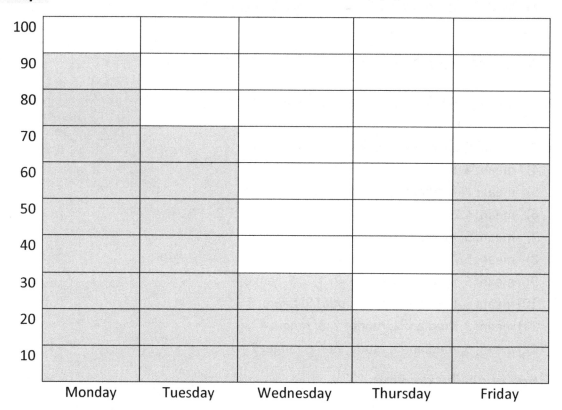

Stem–And–Leaf Plot

1)

Stem	leaf
7	2 4 9 9
8	3 6 8
9	1 5 7

2)

Stem	leaf
1	9
2	6 6 6
3	3 7
4	8 8 9

3)

Stem	leaf
4	1 2
5	3 4 4 8
6	5 5 7 9

The Pie Graph or Circle Graph

1) red
2) 15%
3) black
4) 23%
5) 13%

Scatter Plots

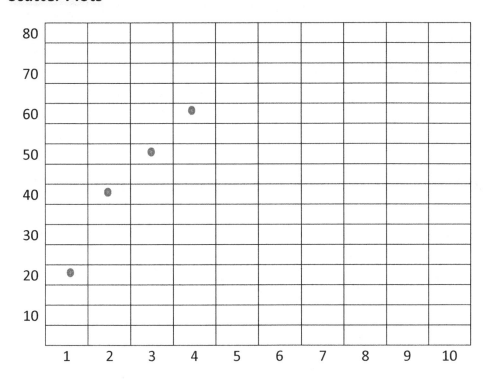

Chapter 15: Geometry

Math Topics that you'll learn today:

✓ The Pythagorean Theorem

✓ Area of Triangles

✓ Perimeter of Polygons

✓ Area and Circumference of Circles

✓ Area of Squares, Rectangles, and Parallelograms

✓ Area of Trapezoids

Mathematics is, as it were, a sensuous logic, and relates to philosophy as do the arts, music, and plastic

art to poetry. — K. Shegel

The Pythagorean Theorem

Helpful

Hints

– In any right triangle:

$a^2 + b^2 = c^2$

Example:

Missing side = 5

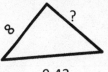

9.43

✍ *Do the following lengths form a right triangle?*

1)

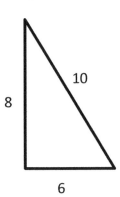

8

10

6

2)

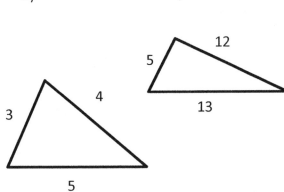

3

4

5

3)

5

12

13

✍ *Find each missing length to the nearest tenth. (all triangles are right triangles)*

4)

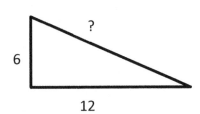

6

?

12

5)

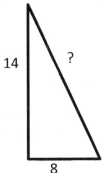

14

?

8

Area of Triangles

Helpful

Hints

Area = $\frac{1}{2}$ (base × height)

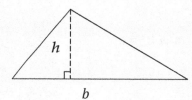

✎ *Find the area of each.*

1)

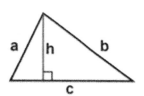

c = 9 mi

h = 3.7 mi

2)

s = 14 m

h = 8 m

3)

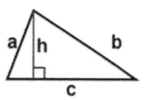

a = 5 m

b = 11 m

c = 14 m

h = 4 m

4)

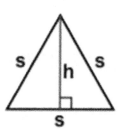

s = 16 m

h = 12.1 m

Perimeter of Polygons

Helpful

Hints

Perimeter of a square = 4s

s

Perimeter of a rectangle

= 2(l + w)

w

l

Perimeter of trapezoid

= a + b + c + d

a

d b

c

Perimeter of Pentagon = 6a

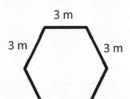

a

Perimeter of a parallelogram = 2(l + w)

l

w

Example:

P = 18

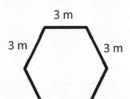

3 m

3 m   3 m

✎ *Find the perimeter of each shape.*

1)
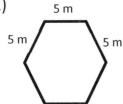

5 m

5 m   5 m

2)
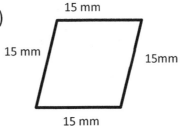

15 mm

15 mm   15mm

15 mm

3)
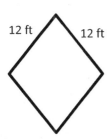

12 ft   12 ft

4)
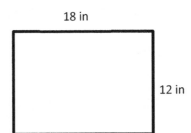

18 in

12 in

Area and Circumference of Circles

Helpful *Hints*	Area = πr² Circumference = 2πr 	**Example:** If the radius of a circle is 3, then: Area = 28.27 Circumference = 18.85

✏️ *Find the area and circumference of each.*

1)

4 in

2)
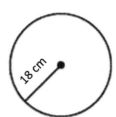
18 cm

3)

5 m

4)
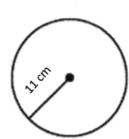
11 cm

5)

8 km

6)
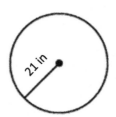
21 in

Area of Squares, Rectangles, and Parallelograms

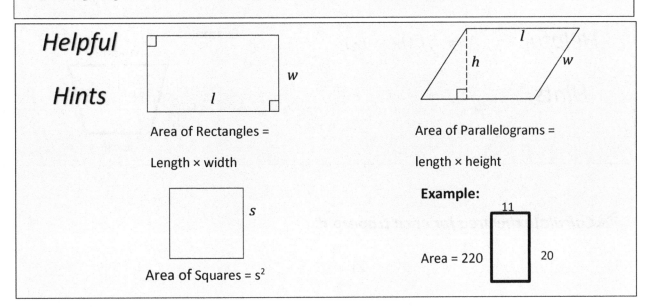

Helpful

Hints

Area of Rectangles =

Length × width

Area of Squares = s^2

Area of Parallelograms =

length × height

Example:

Area = 220

✎ *Find the area of each.*

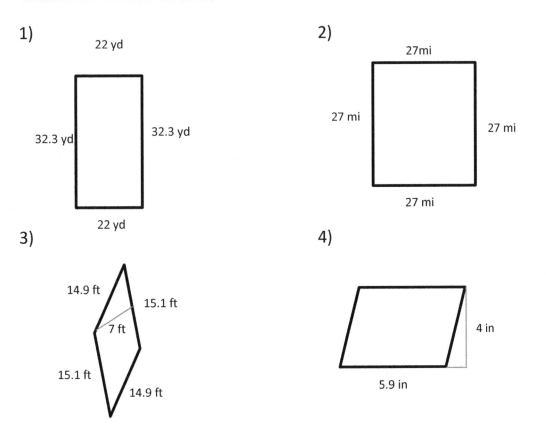

1)

22 yd

32.3 yd   32.3 yd

22 yd

2)

27mi

27 mi   27 mi

27 mi

3)

14.9 ft

15.1 ft

7 ft

15.1 ft

14.9 ft

4)

4 in

5.9 in

Area of Trapezoids

Helpful $A = \frac{1}{2}h(b_1 + b_2)$

Hints

Example:

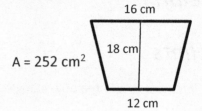

A = 252 cm²

✍️ *Calculate the area for each trapezoid.*

1)

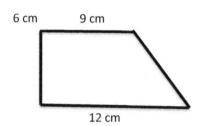

2)

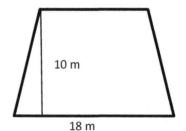

3)

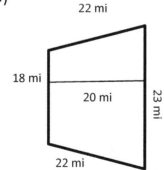

4)

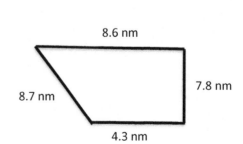

Answers of Worksheets – Chapter 15

The Pythagorean Theorem

1) yes

2) yes

3) no

4) 13.42

5) 16.12

Area of Triangles

1) 16.65 mi^2

2) 84.8 m^2

3) 24.49m^2

4) 110.85 m^2

Perimeter of Polygons

1) 16.65 mi^2

2) 56 m^2

3) 28m^2

4) 96.8 m^2

Area and Circumference of Circles

1) Area: 50.27 in^2, Circumference: 25.12 in

2) Area: 1,017.36 cm^2, Circumference: 113.04 cm

3) Area: 78.5m^2, Circumference: 31.4 m

4) Area: 379.94 cm^2, Circumference: 69.08 cm

5) Area: 200.96 km^2, Circumference: 50.2 km

6) Area: 1,384.74 km^2, Circumference: 131.88 km

Area of Squares, Rectangles, and Parallelograms

1) 710.6 yd^2

2) 729 mi^2

3) 105.7 ft^2

4) 23.6 in^2

Area of Trapezoids

1) 63 cm^2

2) 160 m^2

3) 410 mi^2

4) 50.31 nm^2

Chapter 16: Solid Figures

Math Topics that you'll learn today:

- ✓ Volume of Cubes
- ✓ Volume of Rectangle Prisms
- ✓ Surface Area of Cubes
- ✓ Surface Area of Rectangle Prisms
- ✓ Volume of a Cylinder
- ✓ Surface Area of a Cylinder

Mathematics is a great motivator for all humans. Because its career starts with zero and it never end

(infinity)

Volume of Cubes

Helpful	– Volume is the measure of the amount of space inside of a solid figure, like a cube, ball, cylinder or pyramid.
Hints	– Volume of a cube = (one side)^3
	– Volume of a rectangle prism: Length × Width × Height

✑ *Find the volume of each.*

1)

2)

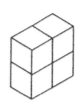

3)

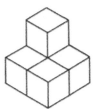

4)

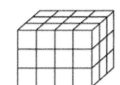

5)

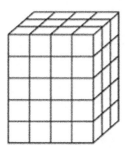

6)

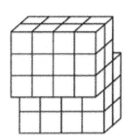

Volume of Rectangle Prisms

Helpful		Example:
	Volume of rectangle prism	$10 \times 5 \times 8 = 400$
Hints	length × width × height	

✎ *Find the volume of each of the rectangular prisms.*

1)

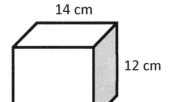

2)

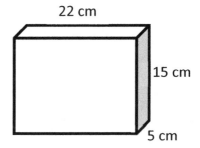

3)

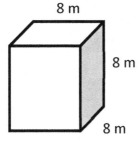

4)

Surface Area of Cubes

Helpful

Hints

Surface Area of a cube =

6 × (one side of the cube)^2

Example:

$6 \times 4^2 = 96m^2$

4 m

4 m

4 m

✎ *Find the surface of each cube.*

1)

6 mm

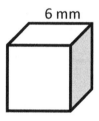

2)

9 mm

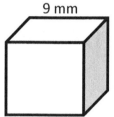

3)

10 cm

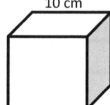

4)

8 m

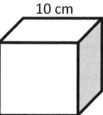

5)

7.5 in

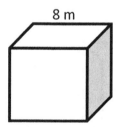

6)

11.3 ft

Surface Area of a Rectangle Prism

Helpful *Hints*	Surface Area of a Rectangle Prism Formula: SA =2 [(width × length) + (height × length) + width × height)]

✍️*Find the surface of each prism.*

1)

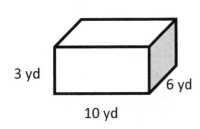

3 yd
10 yd
6 yd

2)

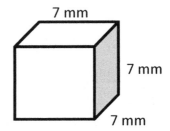

7 mm
7 mm
7 mm

3)

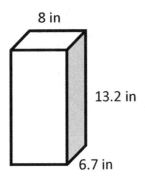

8 in
13.2 in
6.7 in

4)

17 cm

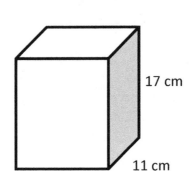

17 cm
11 cm

Volume of a Cylinder

Helpful

Volume of Cylinder Formula = π(radius)^2 × height

Hints

π = 3.14

✒ *Find the volume of each of cubes.*

1)

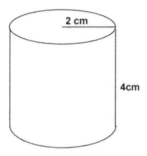
2 cm
4cm

2)

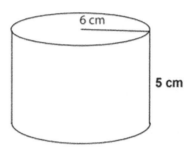
6 cm
5 cm

3)

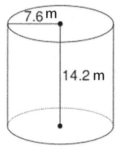
7.6 m
14.2 m

4)

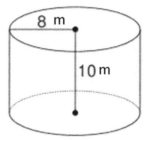
8 m
10 m

Surface Area of a Cylinder

<table>
<tr>
<td>

Helpful

Hints

</td>
<td>

Surface area of a cylinder

SA = 2πr² + 2πrh

</td>
<td>

Example:

Surface area

= 1727

11 m

14 m

</td>
</tr>
</table>

✏️*Find the surface of each cylinder.*

1)

8 ft

8 ft

2)

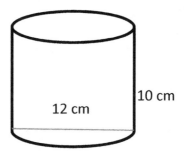

12 cm

10 cm

3)

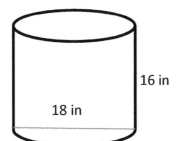

16 in

18 in

4)

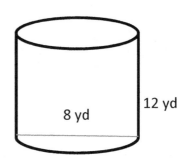

8 yd

12 yd

Answers of Worksheets – Chapter 16

Volumes of Cubes

1) 8

2) 4

3) 5

4) 36

5) 60

6) 44

Volume of Rectangle Prisms

1) 1344 cm^3

2) 1650 cm^3

3) 512 m^3

4) 1144 cm^3

Surface Area of a Cube

1) 216 mm^2

2) 486 mm^2

3) 600 cm^2

4) 384 m^2

5) 337.5 in^2

6) 766.14 ft^2

Surface Area of a Prism

1) 216 yd^2

2) 294 mm^2

3) 495.28 in^2

4) 1326 cm^2

Volume of a Cylinder

1) 50.24 cm^3

2) 5665.2 cm^3

3) 2575.4 m^2

4) 2009.6 m^2

Surface Area of a Cylinder

1) 301.59 ft^2

2) 603.19 cm^2

3) 1413.72 in^2

4) 402.12 yd^2

Chapter 17: Logarithms

Math Topics that you'll learn today:

- ✓ Rewriting logarithms
- ✓ Evaluating logarithms
- ✓ Properties of logarithms
- ✓ Natural logarithms
- ✓ Solving exponential equations requiring logarithms
- ✓ Solving logarithmic equations

Mathematics is an art of human understanding. — William Thurston

Rewriting logarithms

Helpful	$\log_b y = x$	**Example:**
	is equivalent to	$\log_4 y = 3$
Hints	$y = b^x$	$y = 4^3$

Rewrite each equation in exponential form.

1) $\log_{24} 15 = 0.85$

$15 = 24^{0.85}$

3) $\log_7 49 = 2$

$49 = 7^2$

2) $\log_{320} 35 = 0.61$

$35 = 320^{0.61}$

4) $\log_6 36 = 2$

$36 = 6^2$

Rewrite each equation in exponential form.

5) $\log_a \frac{5}{8} = b$

$\frac{5}{8} = a^b$

8) $\log_y x = -8$

$x = y^8$

6) $\log_x y = 6$

$y = x^6$

9) $\log_a b = 22$

$b = a^{22}$

7) $\log_{12} n = m$

$n = 12^m$

10) $\log_{\frac{1}{5}} v = u$

$v = \frac{1}{5}^u$

Evaluate each expression.

11) $\log_4 64 = 3$

13) $\log_5 125 = 3$

12) $\log_4 16 = 2$

14) $\log_9 3 = \frac{1}{2}$

Evaluating logarithms

Helpful	Change of Base Formula:
Hints	$\log_b(x) = \dfrac{\log_d(x)}{\log_d(b)}$

Evaluate each expression.

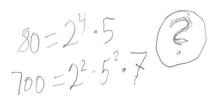

$80 = 2^4 \cdot 5$

$700 = 2^2 \cdot 5^2 \cdot 7$

$7^2 \cdot 7^3 = 7^5$

$7^2 \cdot 7^{-2} = 1$

$7^2 \cdot 7^{-1} = 7^1$

$49 \times \frac{1}{49} = 1$

$10^{-2} = \frac{1}{100}$

$(5^2)^3 = 5^6$

$(5^{\frac{1}{2}})^2 = 5$

1) $\log_3 27 = 3$

2) $\log_2 32 = 5$

3) $\log_4 16 = 2$

4) $\log_2 4 = 2$

5) $\log_8 64 = 2$

6) $\log_7 \frac{1}{49} = -2$

7) $\log_{64} \frac{1}{4} = -\frac{1}{3}$

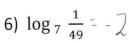

Well done, ma'am!

8) $\log_{80} 700$

9) $\log_4 \frac{1}{64} = -3$

10) $\log_5 625 = 4$

11) $\log_6 216 = 3$

$3 \times 72 = 3^3 \cdot 2^3$

12) $\log_8 \frac{1}{216}$

$2^6 = 64, 2^7 = 1, 512 = 2^9$

13) $\log_8 512 = 3$

49×7

14) $\log_7 2401 = 4$

Properties of logarithms

Helpful	$a^{\log_a b} = b$	$\log_a \frac{1}{x} = -\log_a x$
	$\log_a 1 = 0$	$\log_a x^p = p \log_a x$
Hints	$\log_a a = 1$	$\log_{x^k} x = \frac{1}{x} \log_a x$, for $k \neq 0$
	$\log_a (x \cdot y) = \log_a x + \log_a y$	$\log_a x = \log_{a^c} x^c$
	$\log_a \frac{x}{y} = \log_a x - \log_a y$	$\log_a x = \frac{1}{\log_x a}$

Expand each logarithm.

1) $\log \left(\frac{2}{5}\right)^3$

2) $\log (2 \cdot 3^4)$

3) $\log \left(\frac{5}{7}\right)^4$

4) $\log \frac{2^3}{7}$

5) $\log (x \cdot y)^5$

6) $\log (8 \cdot 5)$

7) $\log (3 \cdot 7)$

8) $\log (x^3 \cdot y \cdot z^4)$

9) $\log \frac{u^4}{v}$

10) $\log \frac{x}{y^6}$

Condense each expression to a single logarithm.

11) $\log 2 - \log 9$

12) $5 \log 6 - 3 \log 4$

13) $\log 7 - 2 \log 12$

14) $4 \log_5 a + 7 \log_5 b$

15) $2\log_3 x - 9 \log_3 y$

16) $\log_4 u - 6 \log_4 v$

17) $4 \log_6 u + 8 \log_6 v$

18) $4 \log_3 u - 20 \log_3 v$

Natural logarithms

Helpful	$\ln(x \cdot y) = \ln(x) + \ln(y)$
	$\ln\left(\dfrac{x}{y}\right) = \ln(x) - \ln(y)$
Hints	$\ln(x^y) = y \cdot \ln(x)$

Solve.

1) $e^x = 3$

2) $\ln(\ln x) = 5$

3) $e^x = 9$

4) $\ln(2x + 5) = 4$

5) $\ln(6x - 1) = 1$

6) $\ln x = \dfrac{1}{2}$

7) $x = e^{\frac{1}{2}}$

8) $\ln x = \ln 4 + \ln 7$

Evaluate without using a calculator.

9) $\ln 1$

10) $\ln e^3$

11) $4 \ln e$

12) $\ln\left(\dfrac{1}{e}\right)$

13) $e^{\ln 10}$

14) $e^{3\ln 2}$

15) $e^{5\ln 2}$

16) $\ln \sqrt{e}$

Solving exponential equations requiring logarithms

Helpful	if	$b^m = b^n$
Hints	then	$m = n$

Solve each equation.

1) $4^{r+1} = 1$

2) $243^x = 81$

3) $6^{-3v-2} = 36$

4) $3^{2n} = 9$

5) $\dfrac{216^{2a}}{36^{-a}} = 216$

6) $25 \cdot 25^{-v} = 625$

7) $3^{2n} = 9$

8) $(\dfrac{1}{6})^n = 36$

9) $32^{2x} = 8$

10) $2^{-3x} = 2^{x-1}$

11) $2^{2n} = 16$

12) $5^{3n} = 125$

13) $3^{-2k} = 81$

14) $5^{3r} = 5^{-2r}$

15) $10^{3x} = 10000$

16) $25 \cdot 125^{-v} = 625$

17) $\dfrac{125}{25^{-3m}} = 25^{-2m-2}$

18) $2^{-2n} \cdot 2^{n+1} = 2^{-2n}$

Solving logarithmic equations

Helpful	- Convert the logarithmic equation to an exponential equation when it's possible. (If no base is indicated, the base of the logarithm is 10)
Hints	- Condense logarithms if you have more than one log on one side of the equation.
	- Plug in the answers back into the original equation and check to see the solution works.

Solve each equation.

1) $2 \log_7 - 2x = 0$

2) $-\log_5 7x = 2$

3) $\log x + 5 = 2$

4) $\log x - \log 4 = 3$

5) $\log x + \log 2 = 4$

6) $\log 10 + \log x = 1$

7) $\log x + \log 8 = \log 48$

8) $-3 \log_3 (x - 2) = -12$

9) $\log 6x = \log (x + 5)$

10) $\log (4k - 5) = \log (2k - 1)$

11) $\log (4p - 2) = \log (-5p + 5)$

12) $-10 + \log_3 (n + 3) = -10$

13) $\log_9 (x + 2) = \log_9 (x^2 + 30)$

14) $\log_{12} (v^2 + 35) = \log_{12} (-2v - 1)$

15) $\log (16 + 2b) = \log (b^2 - 4b)$

16) $\log_9 (x + 6) - \log_9 x = \log_9 2$

17) $\log_5 6 + \log_5 2x^2 = \log_5 48$

18) $\log_6 (x + 1) - \log_6 x = \log_6 29$

Answers of Worksheets – Chapter 17

Rewriting logarithms

1) $24^{0.85} = 15$

2) $320^{0.61} = 35$

3) $7^2 = 49$

4) $6^2 = 36$

5) $a^b = \dfrac{5}{8}$

6) $x^6 = y$

7) $12^m = n$

8) $y^{-8} = x$

9) $a^{22} = b$

10) $(\dfrac{1}{5})^u = v$

11) 3

12) 2

13) 3

14) $\dfrac{1}{2}$

Evaluating logarithms

1) 3

2) 5

3) 2

4) 2

5) 2

6) −2

7) $-\dfrac{1}{3}$

8) 1.5

9) −3

10) 4

11) 3

12) −3

13) 3

14) 4

Properties of logarithms

1) $3 \log 2 - 3 \log 5$

2) $\log 2 + 4 \log 3$

3) $4\log 5 - 4 \log 7$

4) $3 \log 2 - \log 7$

5) $5 \log x + 5 \log y$

6) $\text{Log } 8 + \log 5$

7) $\text{Log } 3 + \log 7$

8) $3\text{Log } x + \log y + 4 \log z$

9) $4 \log u - \log v$

10) $\text{Log } x - 6 \log y$

11) $\log \dfrac{2}{9}$

12) $\log \dfrac{6^5}{4^3}$

13) $\log \dfrac{7}{12^2}$

14) $\log_5 (a^4 b^7)$

15) $\log_3 \dfrac{x^2}{y^9}$

16) $\log_4 \dfrac{u}{v^6}$

17) $\log_6 (v^8 u^4)$

18) $\log_3 \dfrac{u^4}{v^{20}}$

Natural logarithms

1) $x = \ln 3$

2) $x = e^{e^5}$

3) $x = \ln 9$

4) $x = \dfrac{e^2 - 5}{2}$

5) $x = \dfrac{e + 1}{6}$

6) $\ln(e^{3-x}) = 8$

7) $x = -5$

8) $x = 28$

9) 0

10) 3

11) 4

12) -1

13) 10

14) 8

15) 32

16) $\dfrac{1}{2}$

Solving exponential equations requiring logarithms

1) $-\dfrac{1}{2}$

2) $\dfrac{1}{48}$

3) 95

4) 4000

5) 50

6) 1

7) 6

8) 83

9) 1

10) $\dfrac{1}{4}$

11) 2

12) 1

13) -2

14) 0

15) $\dfrac{4}{3}$

16) $-\dfrac{2}{3}$

17) $-\dfrac{7}{10}$

18) -1

Solving logarithmic equations

1) $\{-\dfrac{1}{2}\}$

2) $\{\dfrac{1}{35}\}$

3) $\{-100\}$

4) $\{20\}$

5) $\{\dfrac{25}{2}\}$

6) $\{5\}$

7) $\{\dfrac{37}{7}\}$

8) $\{84\}$

9) $\{3\}$

10) $\{2\}$

11) $\{\dfrac{7}{9}\}$

12) $\{-2\}$

13) $\{-7, -4\}$

14) $\{-6\}$

15) $\{8, -2\}$

16) $\{6\}$

17) $\{2, -2\}$

18) $\{\dfrac{1}{28}\}$

Chapter 18: Matrices

Math Topics that you'll learn today:

- ✓ Adding and subtracting matrices

- ✓ Matrix multiplications

- ✓ Finding determinants of a matrix

- ✓ Finding inverse of a matrix

- ✓ Matrix equations

Mathematics is an independent world created out of pure intelligence.

— William Woods Worth

Adding and subtracting matrices

Helpful	- We can add or subtract two matrices if they have the same dimensions.
Hints	- For addition or subtraction, add or subtract the corresponding entries, and place the result in the corresponding position in the resultant matrix.

Simplify.

1) $\begin{vmatrix} 2 & -5 & -3 \end{vmatrix} + \begin{vmatrix} 1 & -2 & -3 \end{vmatrix}$

2) $\begin{vmatrix} 3 & 6 \\ -1 & -3 \\ -5 & -1 \end{vmatrix} + \begin{vmatrix} 0 & -1 \\ 6 & 0 \\ 2 & 3 \end{vmatrix}$

3) $\begin{vmatrix} -5 & 2 & -2 \\ 4 & -2 & 0 \end{vmatrix} - \begin{vmatrix} 6 & -5 & -6 \\ 1 & 3 & -3 \end{vmatrix}$

4) $\begin{vmatrix} 4 & 2 \end{vmatrix} + \begin{vmatrix} -2 & -6 \end{vmatrix}$

5) $\begin{vmatrix} 2 \\ 4 \end{vmatrix} + \begin{vmatrix} 5 \\ 6 \end{vmatrix}$

6) $\begin{vmatrix} -4n & n+m \\ -2n & -4m \end{vmatrix} + \begin{vmatrix} 4 & -5 \\ 3m & 0 \end{vmatrix}$

7) $\begin{vmatrix} -6r+t \\ -r \\ 6s \end{vmatrix} + \begin{vmatrix} 6r \\ -4t \\ -3r+2 \end{vmatrix}$

8) $\begin{vmatrix} z-5 \\ -6 \\ -1-6z \\ 3y \end{vmatrix} + \begin{vmatrix} -3y \\ 3z \\ 5+z \\ 4z \end{vmatrix}$

9) $\begin{vmatrix} 8 & 7 \\ -6 & 5 \end{vmatrix} + \begin{vmatrix} 4 & -3 \\ 1 & 13 \end{vmatrix}$

10) $\begin{vmatrix} -13 & 18 & 12 \end{vmatrix} + \begin{vmatrix} 34 & -3 & 9 \end{vmatrix}$

11) $\begin{vmatrix} 2 & -5 & 9 \\ 4 & -7 & 11 \\ -6 & 3 & -17 \end{vmatrix} + \begin{vmatrix} 3 & 4 & -5 \\ 13 & 2 & 5 \\ 4 & -8 & 1 \end{vmatrix}$

12) $\begin{vmatrix} 1 & -7 & 15 \\ 31 & 3 & 18 \\ 22 & 6 & 4 \end{vmatrix} + \begin{vmatrix} 13 & 17 & 5 \\ 3 & 8 & -1 \\ -9 & 2 & 12 \end{vmatrix}$

Matrix multiplication

Helpful **Hints**	- Step 1: Make sure that it's possible to multiply the two matrices (the number of columns in the 1st one should be the same as the number of rows in the second one.) - Step 2: The elements of each row of the first matrix should be multiplied by the elements of each column in the second matrix. - Step 3: Add the products.

Simplify.

1) $\begin{vmatrix} -5 & -5 \\ -1 & 2 \end{vmatrix} \cdot \begin{vmatrix} -2 & -3 \\ 3 & 5 \end{vmatrix}$

2) $\begin{vmatrix} 0 & 5 \\ -3 & 1 \\ -5 & 1 \end{vmatrix} \cdot \begin{vmatrix} -4 & 4 \\ -2 & -4 \end{vmatrix}$

3) $\begin{vmatrix} 3 & 2 & 5 \\ 2 & 3 & 1 \end{vmatrix} \cdot \begin{vmatrix} 4 & 5 & -5 \\ 5 & -1 & 6 \end{vmatrix}$

4) $\begin{vmatrix} -5 \\ 6 \\ 0 \end{vmatrix} \cdot \begin{vmatrix} 3 & -1 \end{vmatrix}$

5) $\begin{vmatrix} 3 & -1 \\ -3 & 6 \\ -6 & -6 \end{vmatrix} \cdot \begin{vmatrix} -1 & 6 \\ 5 & 4 \end{vmatrix}$

6) $\begin{vmatrix} -2 & -6 \\ -4 & 3 \\ 5 & 0 \\ 4 & -6 \end{vmatrix} \cdot \begin{vmatrix} 2 & -2 & 2 \\ -2 & 0 & -3 \end{vmatrix}$

7) $\begin{vmatrix} -4 & -y \\ -2x & -4 \end{vmatrix} \cdot \begin{vmatrix} -4x & 0 \\ 2y & -5 \end{vmatrix}$

8) $\begin{vmatrix} 2 & -5v \end{vmatrix} \cdot \begin{vmatrix} -5u & -v \\ 0 & 6 \end{vmatrix}$

9) $\begin{vmatrix} -1 & 1 & -1 \\ 5 & 2 & -5 \\ 6 & -5 & 1 \\ -5 & 6 & 0 \end{vmatrix} \cdot \begin{vmatrix} 6 & 5 \\ 5 & -6 \\ 6 & 0 \end{vmatrix}$

10) $\begin{vmatrix} 5 & 3 & 5 \\ 1 & 5 & 0 \end{vmatrix} \cdot \begin{vmatrix} -4 & 2 \\ -3 & 4 \\ 3 & -5 \end{vmatrix}$

11) $\begin{vmatrix} -3 & 5 \\ -2 & 1 \end{vmatrix} \cdot \begin{vmatrix} 6 & -2 \\ 1 & -5 \end{vmatrix}$

12) $\begin{vmatrix} 0 & 2 \\ -2 & -5 \end{vmatrix} \cdot \begin{vmatrix} 6 & -6 \\ 3 & 0 \end{vmatrix}$

Finding determinants of a matrix

Helpful	$\begin{bmatrix} a & b \\ c & d \end{bmatrix}$	$|A| = ad - bc$
Hints	$\begin{bmatrix} a & b & c \\ d & e & f \\ g & h & i \end{bmatrix}$	$|A| = a(ei - fh) - b(di - fg) + c(dh - eg)$

Evaluate the determinant of each matrix.

1) $\begin{vmatrix} 0 & -4 \\ -6 & -2 \end{vmatrix}$

2) $\begin{vmatrix} 5 & 3 \\ 6 & 6 \end{vmatrix}$

3) $\begin{vmatrix} -1 & 1 \\ -1 & 4 \end{vmatrix}$

4) $\begin{vmatrix} -9 & -9 \\ -7 & -10 \end{vmatrix}$

5) $\begin{vmatrix} -1 & 8 \\ 5 & 0 \end{vmatrix}$

6) $\begin{vmatrix} 8 & -6 \\ -10 & 9 \end{vmatrix}$

7) $\begin{vmatrix} 2 & -2 \\ 7 & -7 \end{vmatrix}$

8) $\begin{vmatrix} -5 & 0 \\ 3 & 10 \end{vmatrix}$

9) $\begin{vmatrix} 0 & 6 \\ -6 & 0 \end{vmatrix}$

10) $\begin{vmatrix} 0 & 4 \\ 6 & 5 \end{vmatrix}$

11) $\begin{vmatrix} -2 & 5 & -4 \\ 0 & -3 & 5 \\ -5 & 5 & -6 \end{vmatrix}$

12) $\begin{vmatrix} 5 & 3 & 3 \\ -4 & -5 & 1 \\ 5 & 3 & 0 \end{vmatrix}$

13) $\begin{vmatrix} 6 & 2 & -1 \\ -5 & -4 & -5 \\ 3 & -3 & 1 \end{vmatrix}$

14) $\begin{vmatrix} 6 & 5 & -3 \\ -5 & 4 & -2 \\ 1 & -4 & 5 \end{vmatrix}$

15) $\begin{vmatrix} -1 & -8 & 9 \\ 4 & 12 & -7 \\ -10 & 3 & 2 \end{vmatrix}$

Finding inverse of a matrix

Helpful

Hints

$$A = \begin{bmatrix} a & b \\ c & d \end{bmatrix} \qquad A^{-1} = \frac{1}{|A|} \begin{bmatrix} d & -b \\ -c & a \end{bmatrix}$$

Find the inverse of each matrix.

1) $\begin{vmatrix} 3 & -2 \\ -4 & 6 \end{vmatrix}$

2) $\begin{vmatrix} 5 & -8 \\ 6 & -9 \end{vmatrix}$

3) $\begin{vmatrix} 2 & -10 \\ -11 & 8 \end{vmatrix}$

4) $\begin{vmatrix} -9 & -6 \\ -5 & -4 \end{vmatrix}$

5) $\begin{vmatrix} -3 & 3 \\ 8 & 7 \end{vmatrix}$

6) $\begin{vmatrix} -2 & 2 \\ -9 & 8 \end{vmatrix}$

7) $\begin{vmatrix} 3 & -2 \\ -4 & 6 \end{vmatrix}$

8) $\begin{vmatrix} -6 & 11 \\ -4 & 7 \end{vmatrix}$

9) $\begin{vmatrix} -1 & 7 \\ -1 & 7 \end{vmatrix}$

10) $\begin{vmatrix} 1 & -1 \\ -6 & -3 \end{vmatrix}$

11) $\begin{vmatrix} 11 & -5 \\ 2 & -1 \end{vmatrix}$

12) $\begin{vmatrix} 0 & -2 \\ -1 & -9 \end{vmatrix}$

13) $\begin{vmatrix} 0 & 0 \\ -6 & 4 \end{vmatrix}$

14) $\begin{vmatrix} -9 & -9 \\ -2 & -2 \end{vmatrix}$

Matrix equations

Helpful	- In a matrix equation, a variable stands for a matrix.
Hints	- Matrix addition or scalar multiplication can be used to solve a matrix equation.

Solve each equation.

1) $\begin{vmatrix} -1 & 2 \\ -6 & 10 \end{vmatrix} z = \begin{vmatrix} 6 \\ 22 \end{vmatrix}$

2) $3x = \begin{vmatrix} 12 & -12 \\ 21 & -27 \end{vmatrix}$

3) $\begin{vmatrix} 20 & -3 \\ 15 & -3 \end{vmatrix} = \begin{vmatrix} -6 & -5 \\ -5 & -4 \end{vmatrix} x$

4) $Y - \begin{vmatrix} -1 \\ -5 \\ 8 \\ 8 \end{vmatrix} = \begin{vmatrix} -6 \\ 6 \\ -16 \\ 0 \end{vmatrix}$

5) $\begin{vmatrix} -1 & -9 \\ 0 & -1 \end{vmatrix} C = \begin{vmatrix} 11 \\ 2 \end{vmatrix}$

6) $\begin{vmatrix} -1 & -2 \\ 2 & 9 \end{vmatrix} B = \begin{vmatrix} -3 & -5 & 13 \\ 21 & 0 & -36 \end{vmatrix}$

7) $\begin{vmatrix} -1 & 1 \\ 5 & -2 \end{vmatrix} C = \begin{vmatrix} 4 \\ -26 \end{vmatrix}$

8) $\begin{vmatrix} 4 & -2 \\ -7 & 2 \end{vmatrix} C = \begin{vmatrix} -6 \\ 12 \end{vmatrix}$

9) $\begin{vmatrix} 2 & -3 \\ -5 & 5 \end{vmatrix} Z = \begin{vmatrix} -1 \\ 20 \end{vmatrix}$

10) $\begin{vmatrix} -5 \\ 5 \\ -20 \end{vmatrix} = 5B$

11) $\begin{vmatrix} -10 \\ 4 \\ 3 \end{vmatrix} = y - \begin{vmatrix} 7 \\ -5 \\ -11 \end{vmatrix}$

12) $-4b - \begin{vmatrix} 5 \\ 2 \\ -6 \end{vmatrix} = \begin{vmatrix} -33 \\ -2 \\ -22 \end{vmatrix}$

Answers of Worksheets – Chapter 18

Adding and subtracting matrices

1) $\begin{vmatrix} 3 & -7 & -6 \end{vmatrix}$

2) $\begin{vmatrix} 3 & 5 \\ 5 & -3 \\ -3 & 2 \end{vmatrix}$

3) $\begin{vmatrix} -11 & 7 & 4 \\ 3 & -5 & 3 \end{vmatrix}$

4) $\begin{vmatrix} 2 & -4 \end{vmatrix}$

5) $\begin{vmatrix} 7 \\ 10 \end{vmatrix}$

6) $\begin{vmatrix} -4n+4 & n+m-5 \\ -2n+3m & -4m \end{vmatrix}$

7) $\begin{vmatrix} t \\ -r-4t \\ 6s-3r+2 \end{vmatrix}$

8) $\begin{vmatrix} z-5-3y \\ -6+3z \\ -4-5z \\ 3y+4z \end{vmatrix}$

9) $\begin{vmatrix} 12 & 4 \\ -5 & 18 \end{vmatrix}$

10) $\begin{vmatrix} 21 & 15 & 21 \end{vmatrix}$

11) $\begin{vmatrix} -1 & -9 & 14 \\ -9 & -9 & 6 \\ -6 & 11 & -18 \end{vmatrix}$

12) $\begin{vmatrix} 14 & 10 & 20 \\ 34 & 11 & 17 \\ 13 & 8 & 16 \end{vmatrix}$

Matrix multiplication

1) $\begin{vmatrix} -5 & -10 \\ 8 & 13 \end{vmatrix}$

2) $\begin{vmatrix} -10 & -20 \\ 10 & -16 \\ 18 & -24 \end{vmatrix}$

3) Undefined

4) $\begin{vmatrix} -15 & 5 \\ 18 & -6 \\ 0 & 0 \end{vmatrix}$

5) $\begin{vmatrix} -8 & 14 \\ 33 & 6 \\ -24 & -60 \end{vmatrix}$

6) $\begin{vmatrix} 8 & 4 & 14 \\ -14 & 8 & -17 \\ 10 & -10 & 10 \\ 20 & -8 & 26 \end{vmatrix}$

9) $\begin{vmatrix} -7 & -11 \\ 10 & 13 \\ 17 & 60 \\ 0 & -61 \end{vmatrix}$

7) $\begin{vmatrix} 16x - 2y^2 & 5y \\ 8x^2 - 8y & 20 \end{vmatrix}$

10) $\begin{vmatrix} -14 & -3 \\ -19 & 22 \end{vmatrix}$

8) $\begin{vmatrix} -10u & -32v \end{vmatrix}$

11) $\begin{vmatrix} -13 & -19 \\ -11 & -1 \end{vmatrix}$

12) $\begin{vmatrix} 6 & 0 \\ -27 & 12 \end{vmatrix}$

Finding determinants of a matrix

1) −24

2) 12

3) −3

4) 27

5) −40

6) 12

7) 0

8) −50

9) −36

10) −24

11) −51

12) 39

13) −161

14) 139

15) 647

Finding inverse of a matrix

1) $\begin{vmatrix} \dfrac{3}{5} & \dfrac{1}{5} \\ \dfrac{2}{5} & \dfrac{3}{10} \end{vmatrix}$

2) $\begin{vmatrix} -3 & \dfrac{8}{3} \\ -2 & \dfrac{5}{3} \end{vmatrix}$

3) $\begin{vmatrix} -\dfrac{4}{47} & -\dfrac{5}{47} \\ -\dfrac{2}{94} & -\dfrac{1}{47} \end{vmatrix}$

4) $\begin{vmatrix} -\dfrac{2}{3} & 1 \\ \dfrac{5}{6} & -\dfrac{3}{2} \end{vmatrix}$

5) $\begin{vmatrix} -\dfrac{7}{45} & \dfrac{1}{15} \\ \dfrac{8}{45} & \dfrac{1}{15} \end{vmatrix}$

6) $\begin{vmatrix} 4 & -1 \\ \dfrac{9}{2} & -1 \end{vmatrix}$

7) $\begin{vmatrix} \dfrac{3}{5} & \dfrac{1}{5} \\ \dfrac{2}{5} & \dfrac{3}{10} \end{vmatrix}$

8) $\begin{vmatrix} \dfrac{7}{2} & -\dfrac{11}{2} \\ 2 & -3 \end{vmatrix}$

9) No inverse exists

10) $\begin{vmatrix} \frac{1}{3} & -\frac{1}{9} \\ -\frac{2}{3} & -\frac{1}{9} \end{vmatrix}$

11) $\begin{vmatrix} 1 & -5 \\ 2 & -11 \end{vmatrix}$

12) $\begin{vmatrix} \frac{9}{2} & -1 \\ -\frac{1}{2} & 0 \end{vmatrix}$

13) No inverse exists

14) No inverse exists

Matrix equations

1) $\begin{vmatrix} 8 \\ 7 \end{vmatrix}$

2) $\begin{vmatrix} 4 & -4 \\ 7 & -9 \end{vmatrix}$

3) $\begin{vmatrix} 5 & 3 \\ -10 & -3 \end{vmatrix}$

4) $\begin{vmatrix} -7 \\ 1 \\ -8 \\ 8 \end{vmatrix}$

5) $\begin{vmatrix} 7 \\ -2 \end{vmatrix}$

6) $\begin{vmatrix} -3 & 9 & -9 \\ 3 & -2 & -2 \end{vmatrix}$

7) $\begin{vmatrix} -6 \\ -2 \end{vmatrix}$

8) $\begin{vmatrix} -2 \\ -1 \end{vmatrix}$

9) $\begin{vmatrix} -11 \\ -7 \end{vmatrix}$

10) $\begin{vmatrix} -1 \\ 1 \\ -4 \end{vmatrix}$

11) $\begin{vmatrix} -3 \\ -1 \\ -8 \end{vmatrix}$

12) $\begin{vmatrix} 7 \\ 0 \\ 7 \end{vmatrix}$

Chapter 19: Functions Operations

Math Topics that you'll learn today:

- ✓ Relations and functions
- ✓ Function notation
- ✓ Adding and subtracting functions
- ✓ Multiplying and dividing functions
- ✓ Composition of functions

Millions saw the apple fall, but Newton asked why." – Bernard Baruch

Function notation

Helpful Hints	Function notation is the way a function is written. It is meant to be a precise way of giving information about the function without a rather lengthy written explanation. The most popular function notation is $f(x)$ which is read "f of x".	**Example:** $f = 12x$ $f(x)\ 12x$

Write in function notation.

1) $d = 22t$

2) $c = p^2 + 5p + 5$

3) $m = 25n - 120$

4) $y = 2x - 6$

Evaluate each function.

5) $w(x) = 3x + 1$, find $w(4)$

6) $h(n) = n^2 - 10$, find $h(5)$

7) $h(x) = x^3 + 8$, find $h(-2)$

8) $h(n) = -2n^2 - 6n$, find $h(2)$

9) $g(n) = 3n^2 + 2n$, find $g(2)$

10) $g(n) = 10n - 3$, find $g(6)$

11) $g(n) = 8n + 4$, find $g(1)$

12) $h(x) = 4x - 22$, find $h(2)$

13) $h(a) = -11a + 5$, find $h(2a)$

14) $k(a) = 7a + 3$, find $k(a - 2)$

15) $h(x) = 3x + 5$, find $h(6x)$

16) $h(x) = x^2 + 1$, find $h(\frac{x}{4})$

Adding and subtracting functions

Helpful *Hints*	Just like we can add and subtract numbers, we can add and subtract functions. For example, if we had functions f and g, we could create two new functions: $f + g$ and $f - g$.	**Example:** $f(x) = 12x$ $g(x) = x^2 + 3x$ $(f + g)(x) = f(x) + g(x) =$ $12x + x^2 + 3x$ $x^2 + 15x$

Perform the indicated operation.

1) $h(t) = 2t + 1$
   $g(t) = 2t + 2$
   Find $(h - g)(t)$

2) $g(a) = -3^a - 3$
   f(a) = $a^2 + 5$
   Find $(g - f)(a)$

3) $g(x) = 2x - 5$
   $h(x) = 4x + 5$
   Find $g(3) - h(3)$

4) $h(3) = 3x + 3$
   $g(x) = -4x + 1$
   Find $(h + g)(10)$

5) $f(x) = 4x - 3$
   $g(x) = x^3 + 2x$
   Find $(f - g)(4)$

6) $h(n) = 4n + 5$
   g(n) = 3n + 4
   Find $(h - g)(n)$

7) $g(x) = -x^2 - 1 - 2x$
   $f(x) = 5 + x$
   Find $(g - f)(x)$

8) $g(t) = 2t + 5$
   $f(t) = -t^2 + 5$
   Find $(g + f)(t)$

Multiplying and dividing functions

		Example:
Helpful **Hints**	Just like we can multiply and divide numbers, we can multiply and divide functions. For example, if we had functions f and g, we could create two new functions $f \cdot g$, and $\dfrac{f}{g}$.	$f(x) = 2x$ $g(x) = x^2 + x$ $(f \cdot g)(x) =$ $f(x) \cdot g(x) =$ $2x^3 + 2x^2$

Perform the indicated operation.

1) $g(a) = 2a - 1$

   $h(a) = 3a - 3$

   Find $(g \cdot h)(-4)$

2) $f(x) = 2x^3 - 5x^2$

   $g(x) = 2x - 1$

   Find $(f \cdot g)(x)$

3) $g(t) = t^2 + 3$

   $h(t) = 4t - 3$

   Find $(g \cdot h)(-1)$

4) $g(n) = n^2 + 4 + 2n$

   $h(n) = -3n + 2$

   Find $(g \cdot h)(1)$

5) $g(a) = 3a + 2$

   $f(a) = 2a - 4$

   Find $\left(\dfrac{g}{f}\right)(3)$

6) $f(x) = 3x - 1$

   $g(x) = x^2 - x$

   Find $\left(\dfrac{f}{g}\right)(x)$

7) $h(a) = 3a$

   $g(a) = -a^3 - 3$

   Find $\left(\dfrac{h}{g}\right)(a)$

Composition of functions

<table>
<tr>
<td rowspan="2">*Helpful*

Hints</td>
<td>The term "composition of functions" (or "composite function") refers to the combining together of two or more functions in a manner where the output from one function becomes the input for the next function.

The notation used for composition is:$(f \circ g)(x) = f(g(x))$</td>
<td>**Example:**

Using $f(x) = x + 1$ and $g(x) = 2x$, find:
$(f \circ g)(1)$

$(f \circ g)(x) = 2x + 1$

$(f \circ g)(1) = 3$</td>
</tr>
</table>

Using f(x) = 5x + 4 and g(x) = x – 3, find:

1) $f(g(6))$

2) $f(f(8))$

3) $g(f(-7))$

4) $g(f(x))$

Using f(x) = 6x + 2 and g(x) = x – 5, find:

5) $f(g(7))$

6) $f(f(2))$

7) $g(f(3))$

8) $g(g(x))$

Using f(x) = 7x + 4 and g(x) = 2x – 4, find:

9) $f(g(3))$

10) $f(f(3))$

11) $g(f(4))$

12) $g(g(5))$

Answers of Worksheets – Chapter 19

Function Notation

1) $d(t) = 22t$
2) $c(p) = p^2 + 5p + 5$
3) $m(n) = 25n - 120$
4) $f(x) = 2x - 6$
5) 13
6) 15

7) 0
8) −20
9) 16
10) 57
11) 12
12) −8

13) $-22a + 5$
14) $7a - 11$
15) $18x + 5$
16) $1 + \dfrac{1}{16}x^2$

Adding and Subtracting Functions

1) −1
2) $-a^2 - 3a - 8$
3) −16

4) −6
5) −59
6) $n + 1$

7) $-x^2 - 3x - 6$
8) $-t^2 + 2t + 10$

Multiplying and Dividing Functions

1) 135
2) $4x^4 - 12x^3 + 5x^2$
3) −28

4) −7
5) $\dfrac{11}{2}$

6) $\dfrac{3x-1}{x^2-x}$
7) $\dfrac{3a}{-a^2-3}$

Composition of functions

1) 19
2) 224
3) −34
4) $5x + 1$

5) 14
6) 86
7) 15
8) $x - 10$

9) 18
10) 179
11) 60
12) 8

Chapter 20: Probability

Math Topics that you'll learn today:

- ✓ Probability of Simple Events
- ✓ Factorials
- ✓ Permutations
- ✓ Combination

Mathematics is the supreme judge; from its decisions there is no appeal.

–Tobias Dantzig

Probability of Simple Events

Helpful *Hints*	- Probability is the likelihood of something happening in the future. It is expressed as a number between zero (can never happen) to 1 (will always happen). - Probability can be expressed as a fraction, a decimal, or a percent.	**Example:** Probability of a flipped coins turns up 'heads' Is $0.5 = \dfrac{1}{2}$

Solve.

1) Find the probability of choosing a month starts in M.

$\dfrac{1}{6}$

2) Find the probability of selecting a month with 30 days.

$\dfrac{1}{3}$

3) When a button is pressed, a computer program outputs a random odd number greater than 1 and less than 9. You press the button twice.

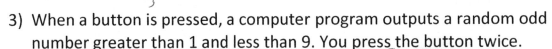

$\{(3,3), (3,5), (3,7), (5,3), (5,5), (5,7), (7,3), (7,5),$

4) The chess club must decide when to meet for a practice. The possible days $(7,7)\}$ are Tuesday, Wednesday, or Thursday. The possible times are 3, 4, or 5 p.m. $\{(T,3), (T,4),$

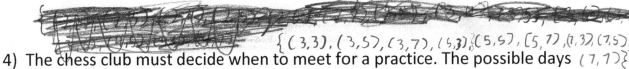

5) The chess club must decide when to meet for a practice. The possible days are Tuesday, Wednesday, or Thursday.

6) A sandwich shop has three types of sandwiches: ham, turkey, and chicken.

7) Three are two boys and girl on a trivia team. Two questions remain. One team member is randomly picked to answer the first question and a different member is picked to answer the second question.

Factorials

| Helpful | Means to multiply a series of descending natural numbers. | **Example:** |
| Hints | | $4! = 4 \times 3 \times 2 \times 1$ |

Determine the value for each expression.

1) $\dfrac{9!}{6!}$

2) $\dfrac{8!}{5!}$

3) $\dfrac{7!}{5!}$

4) $\dfrac{20!}{18!}$

5) $\dfrac{22!}{18!5!}$

6) $\dfrac{10!}{8!2!}$

7) $\dfrac{100!}{97!}$

8) $\dfrac{14!}{10!4!}$

9) $\dfrac{10!}{8!}$

10) $\dfrac{25!}{20!}$

11) $\dfrac{14!}{9!3!}$

12) $\dfrac{55!}{53!}$

13) $\dfrac{(2 \cdot 3)!}{3!}$

14) $5! + 4!$

Permutations

Helpful *Hints*	The number of ways to choose a sample of r elements from a set of n distinct objects where order does matter and replacements are not allowed. $_nP_k = \frac{n!}{(n-k)!}$	**Example:** $_4P_2 = \frac{4!}{(4-2)!}$ $= 12$

Evaluate each expression.

1) $_4P_2$

2) $_5P_1$

3) $_6P_2$

4) $_6P_6$

5) $-4 + _7P_4$

6) $5 \cdot {_6P_5}$

7) $_7P_2$

8) $_4P_1$

9) $_8P_5$

10) $_7P_3$

11) How many possible 7–digit telephone numbers are there? Someone left their umbrella on the subway and we need to track them down.

12) With repetition allowed, how many ways can one choose 8 out of 12 things?

Combination

Helpful *Hints*	The number of ways to choose a sample of r elements from a set of n distinct objects where order does not matter and replacements are not allowed. $_nC_r = \dfrac{n!}{r!\,(n-r)!}$	**Example:** $_4C_2 = \dfrac{4!}{2!(4-2)!}$ = 3

List all possible combinations.

1) 4, 5, 6, 7, taken four at a time

2) T, V, W, taken two at a time

Evaluate each expression.

3) $_7C_5$

4) $_4C_2$

5) $_9C_3$

6) $_5C_2$

7) $_{12}C_8$

8) $_9C_6$

9) $_{22}C_{20}$

10) $_{12}C_8$

11) $_{11}C_8$

12) $_{25}C_{23}$

13) $_{17}C_{10}$

14) $_{24}C_5$

15) $4 \cdot {}_{18}C_{11}$

16) $_{20}C_{16} + 1$

Answers of Worksheets – Chapter 20

Probability of simple events

1) $\frac{1}{6}$ 2) $\frac{1}{3}$

3) {(3, 3), (3, 5), (3, 7), (5, 3), (5, 5), (5, 7), (7, 3), (7, 5), (7, 7)}

4) {(T, 3), (T, 4), (T, 5), (W, 3), (W, 4), (W, 5), (R, 3), (R, 4), (R, 5)}

5) {Tuesday, Wednesday, Thursday}

6) {ham, turkey, chicken}

7) {(B_1, B_2), (B_1, G), (B_2, B_1), (B_2, G), (G, B_1), (G, B_2)}

Factorials

1) 504	6) 45	11) 40,040
2) 336	7) 970,200	12) 2,970
3) 42	8) 1,001	13) 120
4) 380	9) 90	14) 144
5) 1,463	10) 6,375,600	

Permutations

1) 12	5) 836	9) 6,720
2) 5	6) 3, 600	10) 210
3) 30	7) 42	13) 10^7
4) 720	8) 4	14) 12^8

Combination

1) 4567

2) TV VW TW

3) 27

4) 6

5) 84

6) 10

7) 495

8) 84

9) 231

10) 495

11) 165

12) 300

13) 19,448

14) 42,504

15) 127,296

16) 4, 846

17) 11,622

Chapter 21: Trigonometric Functions

Math Topics that you'll learn today:

- ✓ Trig ratios of general angles
- ✓ Sketch each angle in standard position
- ✓ Finding co–terminal angles and reference angles
- ✓ Writing each measure in radians
- ✓ Writing each measure in degrees
- ✓ Evaluating each trigonometric expression
- ✓ Missing sides and angles of a right triangle
- ✓ Arc length and sector area

Mathematics is like checkers in being suitable for the young, not too difficult, amusing, and without peril

to the state. — Plato

Trig ratios of general angles

	θ	0°	30°	45°	60°	90°
Helpful	$\sin\theta$	0	$\dfrac{1}{2}$	$\dfrac{\sqrt{2}}{2}$	$\dfrac{\sqrt{3}}{2}$	1
Hints	$\cos\theta$	1	$\dfrac{\sqrt{3}}{2}$	$\dfrac{\sqrt{2}}{2}$	$\dfrac{1}{2}$	0
	$\tan\theta$	0	$\dfrac{\sqrt{3}}{3}$	1	$\sqrt{3}$	undefined

Use a calculator to find each. Round your answers to the nearest ten–thousandth.

1) $\sin-120°$

2) $\sin 150°$

3) $\cos 315°$

4) $\cos 180°$

5) $\sin 120°$

6) $\sin-330°$

Find the exact value of each trigonometric function. Some may be undefined.

7) $\sec 0$

8) $\tan-\dfrac{3\pi}{2}$

9) $\cos\dfrac{11\pi}{6}$

10) $\cot\dfrac{5\pi}{3}$

11) $\sec-\dfrac{3\pi}{4}$

12) $\tan\dfrac{2\pi}{3}$

Sketch each angle in standard position

Helpful	- The standard position of an angle is when its vertex is located at the origin and its initial side extends along the positive x-axis.
Hints	- A positive angle is the angle measured in a counterclockwise direction from the initial side to the terminal side.
	- A negative angle is the angle measured in a clockwise direction from the initial side to the terminal side.

Draw the angle with the given measure in standard position.

1) $-120°$

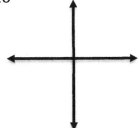

4) $280°$

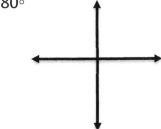

2) $440°$

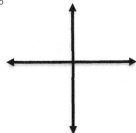

5) $710°$

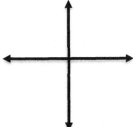

3) $-\dfrac{10\pi}{3}$

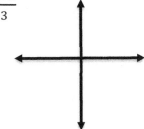

6) $\dfrac{11\pi}{6}$

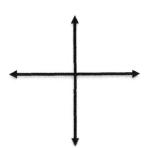

Finding coterminal angles and reference angles

Helpful	- Coterminal angles are equal angles.
	- To find a coterminal of an angle, add or subtract 360 degrees (or 2π for radians) to the given angle.
Hints	- Reference angle is the smallest angle that you can make from the terminal side of an angle with the x-axis.

Find a conterminal angle between 0° and 360°.

1) $-440°$

2) $640°$

3) $-435°$

4) $-330°$

Find a conterminal angle between 0 and 2π for each given angle.

5) $\dfrac{15}{4}$

6) $-\dfrac{19\pi}{12}$

7) $-\dfrac{35}{18}$

8) $\dfrac{11\pi}{3}$

Find the reference angle.

9)

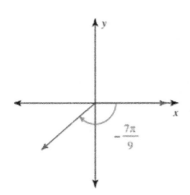

$-\dfrac{7\pi}{9}$

10)

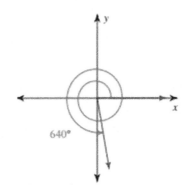

$640°$

Writing each measure in radians

Helpful	$radians = degrees \times \dfrac{\pi}{180}$	**Example:** Convert 150 degrees to radians.
Hints		$radians = 150 \times \dfrac{\pi}{180} = \dfrac{5\pi}{6}$

Convert each degree measure into radians.

1) −140°

2) 320°

3) 210°

4) 970°

5) −190°

6) 345°

7) 265°

8) 555°

9) 300°

10) 50°

11) 315°

12) 600°

13) 712°

14) −160°

15) −210°

16) 545°

17) −30°

18) 660°

19) −170°

20) 230°

21) 150°

Writing each measure in degrees

Helpful *Hints*	$Degrees = radians \times \dfrac{180}{\pi}$	**Example:** Convert $\dfrac{2\pi}{3}$ to degrees. $\dfrac{2\pi}{3} \times \dfrac{180}{\pi} = \dfrac{360\pi}{3\pi} = 120$

Convert each radian measure into degrees.

1) $\dfrac{\pi}{30}$

2) $\dfrac{32}{40}$

3) $\dfrac{14}{36}$

4) $\dfrac{\pi}{5}$

5) $-\dfrac{10\pi}{8}$

6) $\dfrac{14\pi}{3}$

7) $-\dfrac{16}{3}$

8) $-\dfrac{50\pi}{14}$

9) $\dfrac{11\pi}{6}$

10) $\dfrac{5\pi}{9}$

11) $-\dfrac{\pi}{3}$

12) $\dfrac{13\pi}{6}$

13) $\dfrac{15}{20}$

14) $\dfrac{21\pi}{4}$

15) $-\dfrac{68\pi}{45}$

16) $\dfrac{14}{3}$

17) $-\dfrac{41}{12}$

18) $-\dfrac{17\pi}{9}$

19) $\dfrac{35\pi}{18}$

20) $-\dfrac{3\pi}{2}$

21) $\dfrac{4\pi}{9}$

Evaluating each trigonometric function

Helpful	- Step 1: Draw the terminal side of the angle. - Step 2: Find reference angle. (It is the smallest angle that you can make from the terminal side of an angle with the x-axis.) - Step 3: Find the trigonometric function of the reference angle.
Hints	

Find the exact value of each trigonometric function.

1) $\cos 225°$

2) $\tan \dfrac{7\pi}{6}$

3) $\tan -\dfrac{\pi}{6}$

4) $\cot -\dfrac{7\pi}{6}$

5) $\cos -\dfrac{\pi}{4}$

6) $\cos -480°$

7) $\sin 690°$

8) $\tan 420°$

9) $\cot -495°$

10) $\tan 405°$

Use the given point on the terminal side of angle θ to find the value of the trigonometric function indicated.

11) $\sin \theta; (-6, 4)$

12) $\cos \theta; (2, -2)$

13) $\cot \theta; (-7, \sqrt{15})$

14) $\cos \theta; (-2\sqrt{3}, -2)$

15) $\sin \theta; (-\sqrt{7}, 3)$

16) $\tan \theta; (-11, -2)$

Missing sides and angles of a right triangle

Helpful

Hints

SOH – CAH - TOA

$sine\ \theta = \frac{opposite}{hypotenuse}$, $Cos\ \theta = \frac{adjacent}{hypotenuse}$, $\tan\ \theta = \frac{opposite}{adjacent}$

Find the value of each trigonometric ratio as fractions in their simplest form.

1) tan A

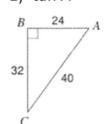

2) sin X

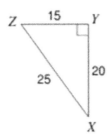

Find the missing side. Round answers to the nearest tenth.

3)

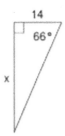

4)

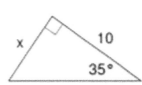

5)

6)

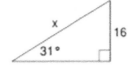

Arc length and sector area

Helpful

Hints

$$Area\ of\ a\ sector = \frac{1}{2}r^2\theta$$

$$length\ of\ a\ sector = (\frac{\theta}{180})\pi r$$

Find the length of each arc. Round your answers to the nearest tenth.

1) r = 28 cm, θ = 45°

3) r = 22 ft, θ = 60°

2) r = 15 ft, θ = 95°

4) r = 12 m, θ = 85°

Find area of a sector. Do not round.

5)

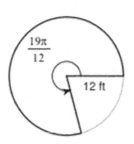

7)

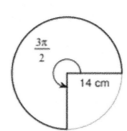

6)

8)

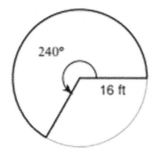

Answers of Worksheets – Chapter 21

Trig ratios of general angles

1) $-\frac{\sqrt{3}}{2}$

2) $\frac{1}{2}$

3) $-\frac{\sqrt{2}}{2}$

4) -1

5) $\frac{\sqrt{3}}{2}$

6) $\frac{1}{2}$

7) 1

8) Undefined

9) $\frac{\sqrt{3}}{2}$

10) $-\frac{\sqrt{3}}{3}$

11) $-\sqrt{2}$

12) $-\sqrt{3}$

Sketch each angle in standard position

1) −120∘

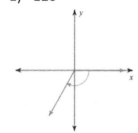

4) 280∘

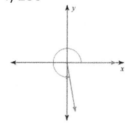

2) 440∘

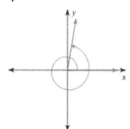

5) 710∘

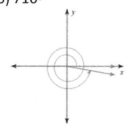

3) $-\frac{10\pi}{3}$

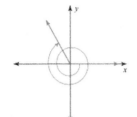

6) $\frac{11\pi}{6}$

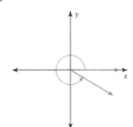

Finding co–terminal angles and reference angles

1) 280°

2) 280°

3) 285°

4) 30°

5) $\frac{7\pi}{4}$

6) $\frac{5\pi}{12}$

7) $\frac{\pi}{18}$

8) $\frac{5\pi}{3}$

9) $\frac{2\pi}{9}$

10) 80°

Writing each measure in radians

1) $-\frac{7\pi}{9}$

2) $\frac{16\pi}{9}$

3) $\frac{7\pi}{6}$

4) $\frac{97}{18}$

5) $-\frac{19\pi}{18}$

6) $\frac{23\pi}{12}$

7) $\frac{53}{36}$

8) $\frac{37}{12}$

9) $\frac{5\pi}{3}$

10) $\frac{5\pi}{18}$

11) $\frac{7\pi}{4}$

12) $\frac{10\pi}{3}$

13) $\frac{178\pi}{45}$

14) $-\frac{8\pi}{9}$

15) $-\frac{7\pi}{6}$

16) $\frac{109\pi}{36}$

17) $-\frac{\pi}{6}$

18) $\frac{11}{3}$

19) $-\frac{17}{18}$

20) $\frac{23}{18}$

21) $\frac{5\pi}{6}$

Writing each measure in degrees

1) 6°

2) 144°

3) 70°

4) 36°

5) −225°

6) 840°

7) −960°

8) −643°

9) 330°

10) 100°

11) −60°

12) 390°

13) 135°

14) 945°

15) −272°

16) 840°

17) −615°

18) −340°

19) 350°

20) −270°

21) 80°

Evaluating each trigonometric expression

1) $-\frac{\sqrt{2}}{2}$

2) $\frac{\sqrt{3}}{3}$

3) $-\frac{\sqrt{3}}{3}$

4) $-\sqrt{3}$

5) $\frac{\sqrt{2}}{2}$

6) $-\frac{1}{2}$

7) $-\frac{1}{2}$

8) $\sqrt{3}$

9) 1

10) 1

11) $\frac{2\sqrt{13}}{13}$

12) $-\sqrt{2}$

13) $-\frac{7\sqrt{15}}{15}$

14) $-\frac{\sqrt{3}}{2}$

15) $\frac{3}{4}$

16) $\frac{2}{11}$

Missing sides and angles of a right triangle

1) $\frac{4}{3}$

2) $\frac{3}{5}$

3) 31.4

4) 7.0

5) 16.2

6) 31.1

Arc length and sector area

1) 22 cm

2) 25 ft

3) 23 ft

4) 18 m

5) 114π ft²

6) $\frac{343\pi}{2}$ in²

7) 147π cm²

8) $\frac{512\pi}{3}$ ft²

PSAT Mathematics
Practice Tests

The Preliminary SAT/National Merit Scholarship Qualifying Test (PSAT/NMSQT) is a standardized test used for college admissions in the United States. 10th and 11th graders take the PSAT to practice for the SAT and to secure a National Merit distinction or scholarship.

The PSAT is similar to the SAT in both format and content. There are three sections on the PSAT:

- Reading
- Mathematics
- Writing

The PSAT Mathematics section is divided into two subsections:

A **No Calculator Section** contains 17 questions and students cannot use a calculator. Students have 25 minutes to complete this section.

A **Calculator Section** contains 31 questions. Students have 45 minutes to complete this section.

40 questions are multiple choice questions and 8 questions are grid-ins.

PSAT Mathematics cover the following topics:

- Pre-Algebra

- Algebra

- Coordinate Geometry

- Plane Geometry

- Date analysis and basic Statistics

- Trigonometry

In this section, there are two complete PSAT Mathematics Tests. Take these tests to see what score you'll be able to receive on a real PSAT test.

Good luck!

Time to Test

Time to refine your skill with a practice examination

Take practice PSAT Math Tests to simulate the test day experience. After you've finished, score your tests using the answer keys.

Before You Start

- You'll need a pencil and a calculator to take the tests.

- It's okay to guess. You won't lose any points if you're wrong.

- After you've finished the test, review the answer key to see where you went wrong.

Mathematics is like love; a simple idea, but it can get complicated.

PSAT Mathematics
Practice Test 1

Section 1

(No Calculator)

17 questions

Total time for this section: 25 Minutes

You may NOT use a calculator on this Section.

Reference Sheet

    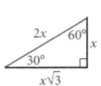

$A = \pi r^2$ $A = \ell w$ $A = \frac{1}{2} bh$ $c^2 = a^2 + b^2$ Special Right Triangles

$C = 2\pi r$

$V = \ell w h$ $V = \pi r^2 h$ $V = \frac{4}{3} \pi r^3$ $V = \frac{1}{3} \pi r^2 h$ $V = \frac{1}{3} \ell w h$

The number of degrees of arc in a circle is 360.

The number of radians of arc in a circle is 2π.

The sum of the measures in degrees of the angles of a triangle is 180.

1) A taxi driver earns $9 per 1-hour work. If he works 10 hours a day and in 1 hour he uses 2-liters petrol with price $1 for 1-liter. How much money does he earn in one day?

    A. $90

    B. $88

    C. $70

    D. $60

2) Five years ago, Amy was three times as old as Mike was. If Mike is 10 years old now, how old is Amy?

    A. 4

    B. 8

    C. 12

    D. 20

3) What is the solution of the following system of equations?
$$\begin{cases} \dfrac{-x}{2} + \dfrac{y}{4} = 1 \\ \dfrac{-5y}{6} + 2x = 4 \end{cases}$$

    A. $x = 48, y = 22$

    B. $x = 50, y = 20$

    C. $x = 20, y = 50$

    D. $x = 22, y = 48$

4) What is the length of AB in the following figure if AE = 4, CD = 6 and AC = 12?

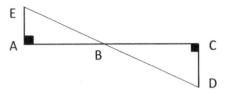

A. 3.8

B. 4.8

C. 7.2

D. 24

5) If a and b are solutions of the following equation, which of the following is the ratio $\frac{a}{b}$?

$(a > b)$

$$2x^2 - 11x + 8 = -3x + 18$$

A. $\frac{1}{5}$

B. 5

C. $-\frac{1}{5}$

D. -5

6) How many tiles of 8 cm² is needed to cover a floor of dimension 6 cm by 24 cm?

A. 6

B. 12

C. 18

D. 24

7) Which of the following is the solution of the following inequality?

$$2x + 4 > 11x - 12.5 - 3.5x$$

A. $x < 3$

B. $x > 3$

C. $x \leq 4$

D. $x \geq 4$

8) If a, b and c are positive integers and $3a = 4b = 5c$, then the value of $a + 2b + 15c$ is how many times the value of a?

A. 11.5

B. 12

C. 12.5

D. 15

9) A company pays its employer $7000 plus 2% of all sales profit. If x is the number of all sales profit, which of the following represents the employer's revenue?

A. $0.02x$

B. $0.98x - 7000$

C. $0.02x + 7000$

D. $0.98x + 7000$

10) If $f(x^2) = 3x + 4$, for all positive value of x, what is the value of $f(121)$?

    A. 367

    B. 37

    C. 29

    D. -29

11) $\dfrac{5x^2 + 75x - 80}{x^2 - 1}$?

    A. $\dfrac{5x + 75}{x - 1}$

    B. $\dfrac{x + 16}{x + 1}$

    C. $\dfrac{5x + 80}{x + 1}$

    D. $\dfrac{x + 15}{x - 1}$

12) If $x^2 + 6x - r$ is divisible by $(x - 5)$, what is the value of r?

    A. 55

    B. 56

    C. 57

    D. 58

13) If a parabola with equation $y = ax^2 + 5x + 10$, where a is constant passes through point (2, 12), what is the value of a^2?

    A. -2

    B. 2

    C. -4

    D. 4

14) In the following equation, what is the value of $y - 3x$?

$$\frac{y}{4} = x - \frac{2}{5}x + 10$$

15) What is the value of x in the following equation?

$$\frac{x^2 - 9}{x + 3} + 2(x + 4) = 15$$

16) If $x \neq 0$, what is the value of $\frac{(10(x)(y^2))^2}{(8xy^2)^2}$?

17) What is the slope of a line containing the reflected points of $A(2, -1)$ and $B(1, 3)$ over the line $y = x$?

The End of Section 1

PSAT Mathematics
Practice Test 1

Section 2

(Calculator)

31 questions

Total time for this section: 45 Minutes

You can use a scientific calculator on this Section.

1) If a car has 80-liter petrol and after one hour driving the car use 6-liter petrol, how much petrol will remain after x-hours driving?

   A. $6x - 80$

   B. $80 + 6x$

   C. $80 - 6x$

   D. $80 - x$

2) 5 less than twice a positive integer is 83. What is the integer?

   A. 39

   B. 41

   C. 42

   D. 44

3) The following graph shows the mark of six students in mathematics. What is the mean (average) of the marks?

   A. 15

   B. 14.5

   C. 14

   D. 13.5

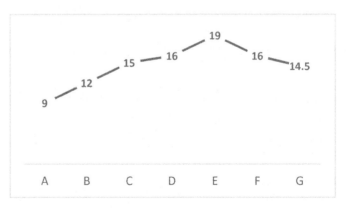

4) The area of a circle is 64π. What is the circumference of the circle?

A. 8 π

B. 16 π

C. 32 π

D. 64 π

5) Which of the following values for x and y satisfy the following system of equations?

$$\begin{cases} x + 4y = 10 \\ 5x + 10y = 20 \end{cases}$$

A. $x = 3, y = 2$

B. $x = 2, y - 3$

C. $x = -2, y = 3$

D. $x = 3, y = -2$

6) If $a \neq 0$ and $6b = 5a\sqrt{3}$, then what is the value of $\frac{2b\sqrt{3}}{4a}$?

A. $\frac{5}{4}$

B. $\frac{5}{4}a$

C. $2a$

D. $2a\sqrt{3}$

7) If a gas tank can hold 25 gallons, how many gallons does it contain when it is $\frac{2}{5}$ full?

    A. 50

    B. 125

    C. 62.5

    D. 10

8) In the xy-plane, the point $(4, 3)$ and $(3, 2)$ are on line A. Which of the following equations of lines is parallel to line A?

    A. $y = 3x$

    B. $y = \frac{x}{2}$

    C. $y = 2x$

    D. $y = x$

9) In the following graph, which of the data point is farthest from the line of best fit (not shown)?

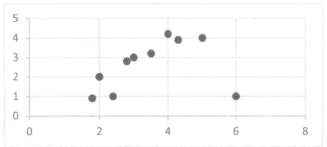

A. $(6, 1)$

B. $(5, 4)$

C. $(3, 3)$

D. $(2, 2)$

10) A football team won exactly 80% of the games it played during last session. Which of the following could be the total number of games the team played last season?

A. 49

B. 35

C. 12

D. 32

11) If x is greater than 0 and less than 1, which of the following is true?

A. $x < \sqrt{x^2 + 1} < \sqrt{x^2} + 1$

B. $x < \sqrt{x^2} + 1 < \sqrt{x^2 + 1}$

C. $\sqrt{x^2 + 1} < x < \sqrt{x^2} + 1$

D. $\sqrt{x^2} + 1 < \sqrt{x^2 + 1} < x$

12) If x is directly proportional to the square of y, and $y = 2$ when $x = 12$, then when $x = 75$

$y = ?$

A. $\frac{1}{5}$

B. 1

C. 5

D. 12

13) Jack earns \$616 for his first 44 hours of work in a week and is then paid 1.5 times his regular hourly rate for any additional hours. This week, Jack needs \$826 to pay his rent, bills and other expenses. How many hours must he work to make enough money in this week?

A. 40

B. 48

C. 53

D. 54

Questions 14 and 16 are based on the following data

Types of air pollutions in 10 cities of a country

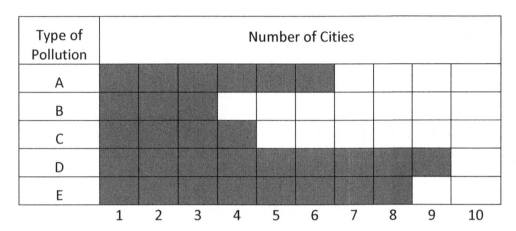

14) If a is the mean (average) of the number of cities in each pollution type category, b is the

   mode, and c is the median of the number of cities in each pollution type category, then

   which of the following must be true?

   A. $a < b < c$
   B. $b < a < c$
   C. $a = c$
   D. $b < c = a$

15) What percent of cities are in the type of pollution A, C, and E respectively?

   A. 60%, 40%, 90%
   B. 30%, 40%, 90%
   C. 30%, 40%, 60%
   D. 40%, 60%, 90%

16) How many cities should be added to type of pollutions B until the ratio of cities in type of pollution B to cities in type of pollution E will be 0.625?

    A. 2

    B. 3

    C. 4

    D. 5

17) The ratio of boys and girls in a class is 4:7. If there are 44 students in the class, how many more boys should be enrolled to make the ratio 1:1?

    A. 8

    B. 10

    C. 12

    D. 16

18) In the following right triangle, if the sides AB and AC become twice longer, what will be the ratio of the perimeter of the triangle to its area?

    A. $\frac{1}{2}$

    B. 2

    C. $\frac{1}{3}$

    D. 3

19) The capacity of a red box is 20% bigger than the capacity of a blue box. If the red box can hold 30 equal sized books, how many of the same books can the blue box hold?

    A. 9

    B. 15

    C. 21

    D. 25

20) The sum of six different negative integers is -70. If the smallest of these integers is -15, what is the largest possible value of one of the other five integers?

    A. -14

    B. -10

    C. -5

    D. -1

21) What is the ratio of the minimum value to the maximum value of the following function?

$$-2 \leq x \leq 3? \ f(x) = -3x + 1$$

    A. $\dfrac{7}{8}$

    B. $-\dfrac{8}{7}$

    C. $-\dfrac{7}{8}$

    D. $\dfrac{8}{7}$

Questions 22 to 24 are based on the following data

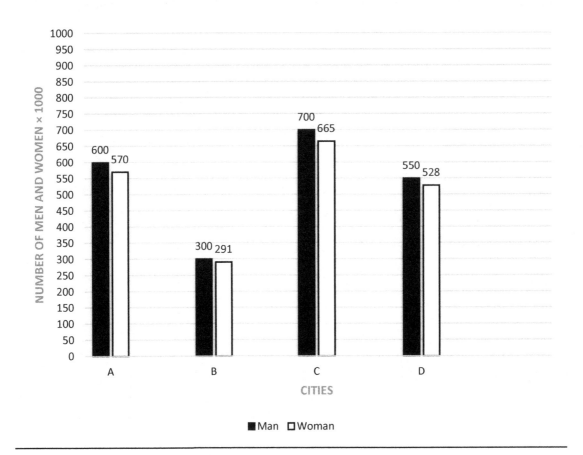

22) What's the maximum ratio of woman to man in the four cities?

A. 0.98

B. 0.97

C. 0.96

D. 0.95

23) What's the ratio of percentage of men in city A to percentage of women in city C?

    A. 0.9

    B. 0.95

    C. 1

    D. 1.05

24) How many women should be added to city D until the ratio of women to men will be 1.2?

    A. 120

    B. 128

    C. 132

    D. 160

25) In the rectangle below if $y > 5$ cm and the area of rectangle is 50 cm^2 and the perimeter of the rectangle is 30 cm, what is the value of x and y respectively?

    A. 4, 11

    B. 5, 11

    C. 5, 10

    D. 4, 10

26) Given the right triangle ABC bellow, $\sin(\beta)$ is equal to?

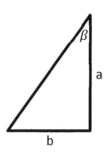

A. $\dfrac{a}{b}$

B. $\dfrac{a}{\sqrt{a^2+b^2}}$

C. $\dfrac{\sqrt{a^2+b^2}}{ab}$

D. $\dfrac{b}{\sqrt{a^2+b^2}}$

27) Solve the following inequality.

$$\left|\frac{x}{2} - 2x + 10\right| < 5$$

A. $-\dfrac{10}{3} < x < 10$

B. $-10 < x < \dfrac{10}{3}$

C. $\dfrac{10}{3} < x < 10$

D. $-10 < x < -\dfrac{10}{3}$

28) $f(x) = ax^2 + bx + c$ is a quadratic function where a, b and c are constant. The value of x of the point of intersection of this quadratic function and linear function $g(x) = 2x - 3$ is 2. The vertex of $f(x)$ is at $(-2, 5)$. What is the product of a, b and c?

29) A ladder leans against a wall forming a 60° angle between the ground and the ladder. If the bottom of the ladder is 30 feet away from the wall, how many feet is the ladder?

30) The volume of cube A is $\frac{1}{2}$ of its surface area. What is the length of an edge of cube A?

31) If $3x + 6y = \frac{-3y^2 + 15}{x}$, what is the value of $(x + y)^2$? $(x \neq 0)$

The End of Section 2

PSAT Mathematics
Practice Test 2

Section 1

(No Calculator)

17 questions

Total time for this section: 25 Minutes

You may NOT use a calculator on this Section.

Reference Sheet

    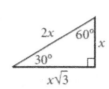

$A = \pi r^2$ $A = \ell w$ $A = \frac{1}{2} bh$ $c^2 = a^2 + b^2$ Special Right Triangles

$C = 2\pi r$

$V = \ell wh$ $V = \pi r^2 h$ $V = \frac{4}{3}\pi r^3$ $V = \frac{1}{3}\pi r^2 h$ $V = \frac{1}{3}\ell wh$

The number of degrees of arc in a circle is 360.

The number of radians of arc in a circle is 2π.

The sum of the measures in degrees of the angles of a triangle is 180.

1) If $3x - 5 = 8.5$, what is the value of $5x + 3$?

    A. 13

    B. 15.5

    C. 20.5

    D. 25.5

2) In a certain bookshelf of a library, there are 35 biology books, 95 history books, and 80 language books. What is the ratio of the number of biology books to the total number of books in this bookshelf?

    A. $\frac{1}{4}$

    B. $\frac{1}{6}$

    C. $\frac{2}{7}$

    D. $\frac{3}{8}$

3) In the figure below, what is the value of x?

    A. 43

    B. 67

    C. 77

    D. 90

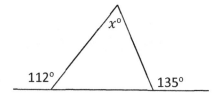

4) The following table represents the value of x and function $f(x)$. Which of the following could be the equation of the function $f(x)$?

A. $f(x) = x^2 - 5$

B. $f(x) = x^2 - 1$

C. $f(x) = \sqrt{x + 2}$

D. $f(x) = \sqrt{x} + 4$

x	$f(x)$
1	5
4	6
9	7
16	8

5) If $xp + 2yq = 26$ and $xp + yq = 17$, what is the value of yq?

A. 6

B. 7

C. 8

D. 9

6) The circle graph below shows all Mr. Green's expenses for last month. If he spent $660 on his car, how much did he spend for his rent?

A. $700

B. $740

C. $780

D. $810

Mr. Green's monthly expenses

7) If $x^2 + 3$ and $x^2 - 3$ are two factors of the polynomial $12x^4 + n$ and n is a constant, what is the value of n?

    A. -108

    B. -24

    C. 24

    D. 108

$$0.ABC \qquad 0.0D$$

8) The letters represent two decimals listed above. One of the decimals is equivalent to $\frac{1}{8}$ and the other is equivalent to $\frac{1}{20}$. What is the product of C and D?

    A. 0

    B. 5

    C. 25

    D. 20

9) The radius of circle A is three times the radius of circle B. If the circumference of circle A is 18π, what is the area of circle B?

A. 3π

B. 6π

C. 9π

D. 12π

10) If the function f is defined by $f(x) = x^2 + 2x - 5$, which of the following is equivalent to $f(3t^2)$?

A. $3t^4 + 6t^2 - 5$

B. $9t^4 + 6t^2 - 5$

C. $3t^4 + 3t^2 - 5$

D. $3t^4 + 6t^2 + 5$

11) In the diagram below, circle A represents the set of all odd numbers, circle B represents the set of all negative numbers, and circle C represents the set of all multiples of 5. Which number could be replaced with y?

A. 5

B. 0

C. -5

D. -10

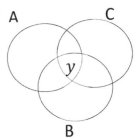

12) There are only red and blue marbles in a box. The probability of choosing a red marble in the box at random is one fourth. If there are 132 blue marbles, how many marbles are in the box?

    A. 140

    B. 156

    C. 176

    D. 190

13) Both $(x = -2)$ and $(x = 3)$ are solutions for which of the following equations?

        I. $x^2 - x + 6 = 0$

        II. $2x^2 - 2x = 12$

        III. $5x^2 - 5x - 30 = 0$

    A. II only

    B. I and II

    C. II and III

    D. I, II and III

14) In the following figure, point O is the center of the circle and the equilateral triangle has perimeter 33. What is the circumference of the circle? ($\pi = 3$)

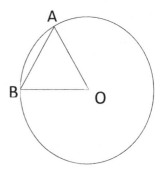

15) If 12% of x is 72 and $\frac{1}{8}$ of y is 16, what is the value of $x - y$?

16) Michelle and Alec can finish a job together in 100 minutes. If Michelle can do the job by herself in 5 hours, how many minutes does it take Alec to finish the job?

17) In the xy-plane, the equation of a line is $ax + by = 4$, where a and b are constant. If that line intersects the x-axis, where x is 4, what is the value of a?

The End of Section 1

PSAT Mathematics
Practice Test 2

Section 2

(Calculator)

31 questions

Total time for this section: 45 Minutes

You can use a scientific calculator on this Section.

1) The Jackson Library is ordering some bookshelves. If x is the number of bookshelf the library wants to order, which each costs $100 and there is a one-time delivery charge of $800, which of the following represents the total cost, in dollar, per bookshelf?

   A. $100x + 800$

   B. $100 + 800x$

   C. $\frac{100x + 800}{100}$

   D. $\frac{100x + 800}{x}$

2) What is the sum of $\sqrt{x-7}$ and $\sqrt{x}-7$ when $\sqrt{x} = 4$?

   A. -3

   B. -1

   C. 0

   D. 3

3) In the following figure, point Q lies on line n, what is the value of y if $x = 35$?

   A. 15

   B. 25

   C. 35

   D. 45

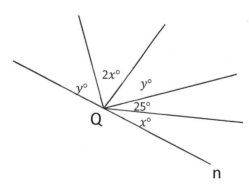

4) In the following figure, AB is the diameter of the circle. What is the circumference of the circle?

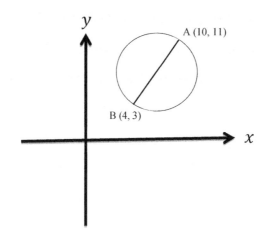

A. 5π

B. 10π

C. 15π

D. 20π

5) What is the smallest integer whose square root is greater than 6?

A. 16

B. 25

C. 37

D. 49

6) What is the value of $\frac{3a-2}{2}$, if $-3a + 5a + 7a = 45$?

A. 6.5

B. 6

C. 5.5

D. 5

7) What is the average (arithmetic mean) of all integers from 11 to 19?

   A. 14

   B. 14.5

   C. 15

   D. 15.5

8) What is the value of $|-12 - 5| - |-8 + 2|$?

   A. 11

   B. -11

   C. 23

   D. -23

9) The table represents different values of function $g(x)$. What is the value of $3g(-2) - 2g(3)$?

   A. -12

   B. -2

   C. 3

   D. 13

x	$g(x)$
-2	3
-1	2
0	1
1	0
2	-1
3	-2

10) A container holds 3.5 gallons of water when it is $\frac{7}{24}$ full. How many gallons of water does the container hold when it's full?

    A. 8

    B. 12

    C. 16

    D. 20

11) If $(3^a)^b = 81$, then what is the value of ab?

    A. 2

    B. 3

    C. 4

    D. 5

12) If the area of the following rectangular ABCD is 100, and E is the midpoint of AB, what is the area of the shaded part?

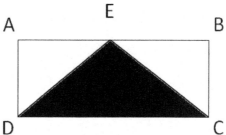

    A. 25

    B. 50

    C. 75

    D. 80

13) Which of the following is equivalent to $13 < -3x - 2 < 22$?

    A. $-8 < x < -5$

    B. $5 < x < 8$

    C. $\frac{11}{3} < x < \frac{20}{3}$

    D. $\frac{-20}{3} < x < \frac{-11}{3}$

Questions 14 to 16 are based on the following data

Number of clothes sold in a clothing store

14) Between which two of the months shown was there a twenty percent decreased in the number of pants sold?

   A. January and February

   B. February and March

   C. March and April

   D. April and May

15) During the six-month period shown, what is the median number of shirts and mean number of shoes per month?

   A. 146.5, 30

   B. 147.5, 29

   C. 146.5, 31

   D. 147.5, 30

16) How many shoes need to be added in April until the ratio of number of pants to number of shoes in April equals to five-seventeenth of this ratio in May?

   A. 90
   B. 80
   C. 70
   D. 60

17) What is the x-intercept of the line with equation $2x - 2y = 5$?

   A. -5
   B. -2
   C. $\frac{5}{2}$
   D. $\frac{5}{4}$

18) The perimeter of a triangle is 10 cm and the lengths of its sides are different integers. What is the greatest possible value of the biggest side?

   A. 4 cm
   B. 5 cm
   C. 6 cm
   D. 7 cm

19) What is the area of the quadrilateral ABCD?

A. 27

B. 30

C. 33

D. 36

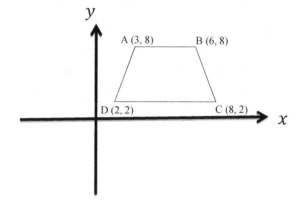

20) If a is an odd integer divisible by 5. Which of the following must be divisible by 4?

A. $a - 1$

B. $a + 1$

C. $2a$

D. $2a - 2$

21) If $(x - 2)^3 = 27$ which of the following could be the value of $(x - 4)(x - 3)$?

A. 1

B. 2

C. −1

D. −2

Questions 22 to 24 are based on the following data

A library has 840 books that include Mathematics, Physics, Chemistry, English and History.

Use following graph to answer questions 15 to 17.

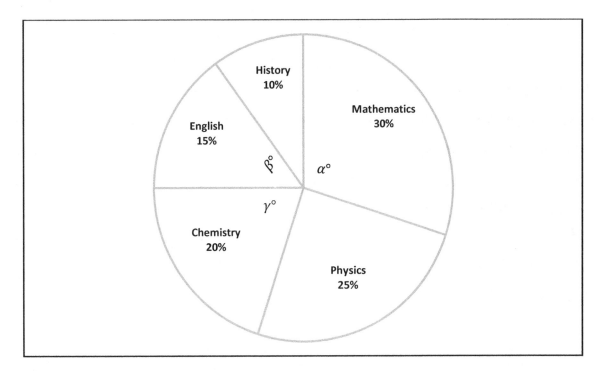

22) What is the product of the number of Mathematics and number of English books?

    A. 21168
    B. 31752
    C. 26460
    D. 17640

23) What are the values of angle α and β respectively?

    A. 90°, 54°
    B. 120°, 36°
    C. 120°, 45°
    D. 108°, 54°

24) The librarians decided to move some of the books in the Mathematics section to Chemistry section. How many books are in the Chemistry section if now $\gamma = \frac{2}{5}\alpha$?

    A. 80
    B. 120
    C. 150
    D. 180

25) In 1999, the average worker's income increased $2,000 per year starting from $24,000 annual salary. Which equation represents income greater than average? (I = income, x = number of years after 1999)

    A. $I > 2000\,x + 24000$

    B. $I > -\,2000\,x + 24000$

    C. $I < -\,2000\,x + 24000$

    D. $I < 2000\,x - 24000$

26) If the area of trapezoid is 126 cm, what is the perimeter of the trapezoid?

    A. 12 cm

    B. 32 cm

    C. 46 cm

    D. 55 cm

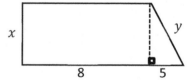

27) What is the solution of the following inequality?

$$|x - 2| \geq 3$$

A. $x \geq 5 \cup x \leq -1$

B. $-1 \leq x \leq 5$

C. $x \geq 5$

D. $x \leq -1$

28) In the following figure, ABCD is a rectangle. If $a = \sqrt{3}$, and $b = 2a$, find the area of the

shaded region? (the shaded region is a trapezoid)

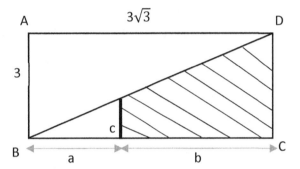

29) If $sin\ A\ =\ \frac{1}{3}$ in a right triangle and the angle A is an acute angle, then what is $cos\ A$?

30) 6 liters of water are poured into an aquarium that's 15cm long, 5cm wide, and 60cm high. How many cm will the water level in the aquarium rise due to this added water? (1 liter of water = 1000 cm³)?

31) If $x \begin{bmatrix} 2 & 0 \\ 0 & 4 \end{bmatrix} = \begin{bmatrix} x + 3y - 5 & 0 \\ 0 & 2y + 10 \end{bmatrix}$, what is the product of x and y?

The End of Section 2

PSAT Mathematics Practice Tests Answers and Explanations

✳ Now, it's time to review your results to see where you went wrong and what areas you need to improve!

PSAT Mathematics Practice Test 1

Section 1 – No Calculator				Section 2 - Calculator			
1-	C	11-	C	1-	C	17-	C
2-	D	12-	A	2-	D	18-	A
3-	D	13-	D	3-	B	19-	D
4-	B	14-	50	4-	B	20-	C
5-	D	15-	10/3	5-	C	21-	B
6-	C	16-	25/16	6-	A	22-	B
7-	A	17-	−1/4	7-	D	23-	D
8-	A			8-	D	24-	C
9-	C			9-	A	25-	C
10-	B			10-	B	26-	D
				11-	A	27-	C
				12-	C	28-	1
				13-	D	29-	60
				14-	C	30-	3
				15-	A	31-	5
				16-	A		

PSAT Mathematics Practice Test 2							
Section 1 – No Calculator				Section 2 - Calculator			
1-	D	11-	C	1-	C	17-	C
2-	B	12-	C	2-	C	18-	A
3-	B	13-	C	3-	B	19-	A
4-	D	14-	66	4-	B	20-	D
5-	D	15-	472	5-	C	21-	B
6-	D	16-	150	6-	A	22-	B
7-	A	17-	1	7-	C	23-	D
8-	C			8-	A	24-	C
9-	C			9-	D	25-	A
10-	B			10-	B	26-	C
				11-	C	27-	A
				12-	B	28-	$4\sqrt{3}$
				13-	A	29-	$\sqrt{8}/3$
				14-	A	30-	80
				15-	D	31-	12
				16-	D		

PSAT Mathematics Practice Tests Explanations

PSAT Mathematics Practice Test 1

Section 1 – No Calculator

1) Choice C is correct

$\$9 \times 10 = \$90$

Petrol use: $10 \times 2 = 20$ liters

Petrol cost: $20 \times \$1 = \$20$

Money earned: $\$90 - \$20 = \$70$

2) Choice D is correct

Five years ago, Amy was three times as old as Mike. Mike is 10 years now. Therefore, 5 years ago Mike was 5 years.

Five years ago, Amy was: $A = 3 \times 5 = 15$

Now Amy is 20 years old: $15 + 5 = 20$

3) Choice D is correct

$\begin{cases} \frac{-x}{2} + \frac{y}{4} = 1 \\ \frac{-5y}{6} + 2x = 4 \end{cases} \rightarrow$ Multiply the top equation by 4. Then,

$\begin{cases} -2x + y = 4 \\ \frac{-5y}{6} + 2x = 4 \end{cases} \rightarrow$ Add two equations.

$\frac{1}{6}y = 8 \rightarrow y = 48$, plug in the value of y into the first equation $\rightarrow x = 22$

4) Choice B is correct

Two triangles ΔBAE and ΔBCD are similar. Then:

$$\frac{AE}{CD} = \frac{AB}{BC} \rightarrow \frac{4}{6} = \frac{x}{12} \rightarrow 48 - 4x = 6x \rightarrow 10x = 48 \rightarrow x = 4.8$$

5) Choice D is correct

$$2x^2 - 11x + 8 = -3x + 18 \rightarrow 2x^2 - 11x + 3x + 8 - 18 = 0 \rightarrow 2x^2 - 8x - 10 = 0$$

$\rightarrow 2(x^2 - 4x - 5) = 0 \rightarrow$ Divide both sides by 2. Then:

$x^2 - 4x - 5 = 0$, Find the factors of the quadratic equation.

$\rightarrow (x - 5)(x + 1) = 0 \rightarrow x = 5 \qquad$ or $\qquad x = -1$

$a > b$, then: $a = 5$ and $b = -1$

$$\frac{a}{b} = \frac{5}{-1} = -5$$

6) Choice C is correct

The area of the floor is: 6 cm × 24 cm = 144 cm

The number is tiles needed = 144 ÷ 8 = 18

7) Choice A is correct

$2x + 4 > 11x - 12.5 - 3.5x \rightarrow$ Combine like terms:

$2x + 4 > 7.5x - 12.5 \rightarrow$ Subtract 2x from both sides: $4 > 5.5x - 12.5$

Add 12.5 both sides of the inequality.

$16.5 > 5.5x$, Divide both sides by 5.5.

$$\frac{16.5}{5.5} > x \rightarrow x < 3$$

8) Choice A is correct

$$3a = 4b \rightarrow b = \frac{3a}{4} \qquad \text{and} \qquad 3a = 5c \rightarrow c = \frac{3a}{5}$$

$$a + 2b + 15c = a + \left(2 \times \frac{3a}{4}\right) + \left(15 \times \frac{3a}{5}\right) = a + 1.5a + 9a = 11.5a$$

9) Choice C is correct

x is the number of all sales profit and 2% of it is:

$$2\% \times x = 0.02x$$

Employer's revenue: $0.2x + 7000$

10) Choice B is correct

$x^2 = 121 \rightarrow x = 11$ (positive value) $\qquad$ Or $\qquad x = -11$ (negative value)

Since x is positive, then:

$$f(121) = f(11^2) = 3(11) + 4 = 33 + 4 = 37$$

11) Choice C is correct

First, find the factors of numerator and denominator of the expression. Then simplify.

$$\frac{5x^2 + 75x - 80}{x^2 - 1} = \frac{5(x^2 + 15x - 16)}{(x - 1)(x + 1)} = \frac{5(x + 16)(x - 1)}{(x - 1)(x + 1)} = \frac{5(x + 16)}{(x + 1)} = \frac{5x + 80}{x + 1}$$

12) Choice A is correct

If $r = 55 \rightarrow \frac{x^2 + 6x - 5}{x - 5} = \frac{(x + 11)(x - 5)}{(x - 5)} = x + 11$

For all other options, the numerator expression is not divisible by $(x - 5)$.

13) Choice D is correct

Plug in the values of x and y in the equation of the parabola. Then:

$$12 = a(2)^2 + 5(2) + 10 \rightarrow 12 = 4a + 10 + 10 \rightarrow 12 = 4a + 20$$

$\rightarrow 4a = 12 - 20 = -8 \rightarrow a = \dfrac{-8}{4} = -2 \rightarrow a^2 = (-2)^2 = 4$

14) The answer is 50

$\dfrac{y}{5} = x - \dfrac{2}{5}x + 10$, Multiply both sides of the equation by 5. Then:

$$5 \times \dfrac{y}{5} = 5 \times \left(x - \dfrac{2}{5}x + 10\right) \rightarrow y = 5x - 2x + 50 \rightarrow y = 3x + 50$$

Now, subtract $3x$ from both sides of the equation. Then:

$$y - 3x = 50$$

15) The answer is $\dfrac{10}{3}$.

First, factorize the numerator and simplify.

$$\dfrac{x^2 - 9}{x + 3} + 2(x + 4) = 15 \rightarrow \dfrac{(x - 3)(x + 3)}{x + 3} + 2x + 8 = 15$$

$\rightarrow x - 3 + 2x + 8 = 15 \rightarrow 3x + 5 = 15$

Subtract 5 from both sides of the equation. Then:

$\rightarrow 3x = 15 - 5 = 10 \rightarrow x = \dfrac{10}{3}$

16) The answer is $\dfrac{25}{16}$.

First, simplify the numerator and the denominator.

$$\dfrac{(10(x)(y^2)^2}{(8xy^2)^2} = \dfrac{100x^2y^4}{64x^2y^4}$$

Remove x^2y^4 from both numerator and denominator.

$$\frac{100x^2y^4}{64x^2y^4} = \frac{100}{64} = \frac{25}{16}$$

17) The answer is $-\frac{1}{4}$ or -0.25.

Remember that, the reflection of the point (x, y) over the line $y = x$ is the point (y, x). Then:

The reflected point of $A(2, -1)$, is $(-1, 2)$

The reflected point of $B(1, 3)$ is point $(3, 1)$

Therefore, the slope of the reflected line is: $\qquad m = \frac{y_2 - y_1}{x_2 - x_1} = \frac{1 - 2}{3 - (-1)} = \frac{-1}{4} \, or - 0.25$

Section 2 –Calculator

1) **Choice C is correct**

The amount of petrol consumed after x hours is: $6 \times x = 6x$

Petrol remaining after x hours driving: $80 - 6x$

2) **Choice D is correct**

Let x be the integer. Then:

$2x - 5 = 83$

Add 5 both sides: $2x = 88$

Divide both sides by 2: $x = 44$

3) **Choice B is correct**

$$average \ (mean) = \frac{sum \ of \ terms}{number \ of \ terms} = \frac{9+12+15+16+19+16 \quad .5}{7} = 14.5$$

4) **Choice B is correct**

Use the formula of areas of circles.

Area of a circle $= \pi r^2 \rightarrow 64 \ \pi = \pi r^2 \rightarrow 64 = r^2 \rightarrow r = 8$

Radius of the circle is 8. Now, use the circumference formula:

Circumference $= 2\pi r = 2\pi \ (8) = 16 \ \pi$

5) **Choice C is correct**

$\begin{cases} x + 4y = 10 \\ 5x + 10y = 20 \end{cases} \rightarrow$ Multiply the top equation by -5 then,

$$\begin{cases} -5x - 20y = -50 \\ 5x + 10y = 20 \end{cases} \rightarrow \quad \text{Add two equations}$$

$-10y = -30 \rightarrow y = 3$, plug in the value of y into the first equation

$$x + 4y = 10 \rightarrow x + 4(3) = 10 \rightarrow x + 12 = 10$$

Subtract 12 from both sides of the equation. Then:

$$x + 12 = 10 \rightarrow x = -2$$

6) Choice A is correct

$$6b = 5a\sqrt{3} \rightarrow b = \frac{5a\sqrt{3}}{6}$$

Therefore: $\quad \dfrac{2b\sqrt{3}}{4a} = \dfrac{2 \times \frac{5a\sqrt{3}}{6} \times \sqrt{3}}{4a} = \dfrac{2 \times 5a \times 3}{4 \times 6a} = \dfrac{5}{4}$

7) Choice D is correct

$$\frac{2}{5} \times 25 = \frac{50}{5} = 10$$

8) Choice D is correct

The slop of line A is: $m = \dfrac{y_2 - y_1}{x_2 - x_1} = \dfrac{3-2}{4-3} = 1$

Parallel lines have the same slope and only choice D $(y = x)$ has slope of 1.

9) Choice A is correct

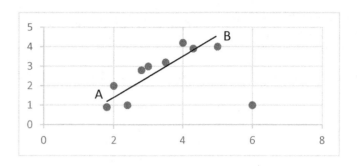

Line AB is the best fit line.

Then, point $(6, 1)$ is the farthest from line AB.

10) Choice B is correct

Choices A, C and D are incorrect because 80% of each of the numbers is non-whole number.

    E. 49, $80\% \ of \ 49 \ = \ 0.80 \times 49 = 39.2$

    F. 35, $80\% \ of \ 35 = 0.80 \times 35 = 28$

    G. 12, $80\% \ of \ 12 = 0.80 \times 12 = 9.6$

    H. 32, $80\% \ of \ 32 = 0.80 \times 32 = 25.6$

11) Choice A is correct

Let x be equal to 0.5, then: $x = 0.5$

$$\sqrt{x^2 + 1} = \sqrt{0.5^2 + 1} = \sqrt{1.25} \approx 1.12$$

$$\sqrt{x^2 + 1} = \sqrt{0.5^2 + 1} = 0.5 + 1 = 1.5$$

Then, option A is correct.

$$x < \sqrt{x^2 + 1} < \sqrt{x^2} + 1$$

12) Choice C is correct

x is directly proportional to the square of y. Then:

$$x = cy^2$$

$$12 = c(2)^2 \rightarrow 12 = 4c \rightarrow c = \frac{12}{4} = 3$$

The relationship between x and y is:

$$x = 3y^2$$

$$x = 75$$

$$75 = 3y^2 \rightarrow y^2 = \frac{75}{3} = 25 \rightarrow y = 5$$

13) Choice D is correct

The amount of money that jack earns for one hour: $\frac{\$616}{44} = \$14$

Number of additional hours that he work to make enough money is: $\frac{\$826 - \$616}{1.5 \times \$14} = 10$

Number of total hours is: $44 + 10 = 54$

14) Choice C is correct

Let's find the mean (average), mode and median of the number of cities for each type of pollution.

Number of cities for each type of pollution: 6, 3, 4, 9, 8

$$average\ (mean) = \frac{sum\ of\ terms}{number\ of\ terms} = \frac{6+3+4+9+8}{5} = \frac{30}{5} = 6$$

Median is the number in the middle. To find median, first list numbers in order from smallest to largest.

3, 4, 6, 8, 9

Median of the data is 6.

Mode is the number which appears most often in a set of numbers. Therefore, there is no mode in the set of numbers.

Median = Mean, then, $a=c$

15) Choice A is correct

Percent of cities in the type of pollution A: $\frac{6}{10} \times 100 = 60\%$

Percent of cities in the type of pollution C: $\frac{4}{10} \times 100 = 40\%$

Percent of cities in the type of pollution E: $\frac{9}{10} \times 100 = 90\%$

16) Choice A is correct

Let the number of cities should be added to type of pollutions B be x. Then:

$$\frac{x+3}{8} = 0.625 \rightarrow x + 3 = 8 \times 0.625 \rightarrow x + 3 = 5 \rightarrow x = 2$$

17) Choice C is correct

The ratio of boy to girls is 4:7. Therefore, there are 4 boys out of 11 students. To find the answer, first divide the total number of students by 11, then multiply the result by 4.

44 ÷ 11 = 4 ⇒ 4 × 4 = 16

There are 16 boys and 28 (44 – 16) girls. So, 12 more boys should be enrolled to make the ratio 1:1

18) Choice A is correct

$AB = 12$ And $AC = 5$

$BC = \sqrt{12^2 + 5^2} = \sqrt{144 + 25} = \sqrt{169} = 13$

Perimeter $= 5 + 12 + 13 = 30$

Area $= \frac{5 \times 12}{2} = 5 \times 6 = 30$

In this case, the ratio of the perimeter of the triangle to its area is: $\frac{30}{30} = 1$

If the sides AB and AC become twice longer, then:

$AB = 24$ And $AC = 10$

$BC = \sqrt{24^2 + 10^2} = \sqrt{576 + 100} = \sqrt{676} = 26$

Perimeter $= 26 + 24 + 10 = 60$

Area $= \frac{10 \times 24}{2} = 10 \times 12 = 120$

In this case the ratio of the perimeter of the triangle to its area is: $\frac{60}{120} = \frac{1}{2}$

19) Choice D is correct

The capacity of a red box is 20% bigger than the capacity of a blue box and it can hold 30 books. Therefore, we want to find a number that 20% bigger than that number is 30. Let x be that number. Then:

$1.20 \times x = 30$, Divide both sides of the equation by 1.2. Then:

$$x = \frac{30}{1.20} = 25$$

Number of books in 30% of red box$= \frac{30}{100} \times 30 = 9 \rightarrow 30 - 9 = 21$

20) Choice C is correct

The smallest number is -15. To find the largest possible value of one of the other five integers, we need to choose the smallest possible integers for four of them. Let x be the largest number. Then:

$$-70 = (-15) + (-14) + (-13) + (-12) + (-11) + x \rightarrow -70 = -65 + x$$

$$\rightarrow x = -70 + 65 = -5$$

21) Choice B is correct

Since $f(x)$ is linear function with a negative slop, then when $x = -2$, $f(x)$ is maximum and when $x = 3$, $f(x)$ is minimum. Then the ratio of the minimum value to the maximum value of the function is: $\frac{f(3)}{f(-2)} = \frac{-3(3)+1}{-3(-2)+1} = \frac{-8}{7} = -\frac{8}{7}$

22) Choice B is correct

Ratio of women to men in city A: $\frac{570}{600} = 0.95$

Ratio of women to men in city B: $\frac{291}{300} = 0.97$

Ratio of women to men in city C: $\frac{665}{700} = 0.95$

Ratio of women to men in city D: $\frac{528}{550} = 0.96$

23) Choice D is correct

Percentage of men in city A $= \frac{600}{1170} \times 100 = 51.28\%$

Percentage of women in city C $= \frac{665}{1365} \times 100 = 48.72\%$

Percentage of men in city A to percentage of women in city C $= \frac{51.28}{48.72} = 1.05$

24) Choice C is correct

Let the number of women should be added to city D be x, then:

$$\frac{528 + x}{550} = 1.2 \rightarrow 528 + x = 550 \times 1.2 = 660 \rightarrow x = 132$$

25) Choice C is correct

The perimeter of the rectangle is: $2x + 2y = 30 \rightarrow x + y = 15 \rightarrow x = 15 - y$

The area of the rectangle is: $x \times y = 50 \rightarrow (15 - y)(y) = 50 \rightarrow y^2 - 15y + 50 = 0$

Solve the quadratic equation by factoring method.

$(y - 5)(y - 10) = 0 \rightarrow y = 5$ (Unacceptable, because y must be greater than 5) or $y = 10$

If $y = 10 \rightarrow x \times y = 50 \rightarrow x \times 10 = 50 \rightarrow x = 5$

26) Choice D is correct

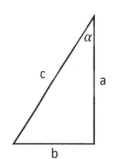

$$\sin \beta = \frac{opposit\ side}{hypotenuse}$$

To find the hypotenuse, we need to use Pythagorean theorem.

$$a^2 + b^2 = c^2 \rightarrow c = \sqrt{a^2 + b^2}$$

$$\sin(\beta) = \frac{b}{c} = \frac{b}{\sqrt{a^2 + b^2}}$$

27) Choice C is correct

$$\left|\frac{x}{2} - 2x + 10\right| < 5 \rightarrow \left|-\frac{3}{2}x + 10\right| < 5 \rightarrow -5 < -\frac{3}{2}x + 10 < 5$$

Subtract 10 from all sides of the inequality.

$$\rightarrow -5 - 10 < -\frac{3}{2}x + 10 - 10 < 5 - 10 \rightarrow -15 < -\frac{3}{2}x < -5$$

Multiply all sides by 2.

$$\rightarrow 2 \times (-15) < 2 \times \left(-\frac{3x}{2}\right) < 2 \times (-5) \rightarrow -30 < -3x < -10$$

Divide all sides by -3. (Remember that when you divide all sides of an inequality by a negative number, the inequality sing will be swapped. $<$ becomes $>$)

$$\to \frac{-30}{-3} > \frac{-3x}{-3} > \frac{-10}{-3}$$

$$\to 10 > x > \frac{10}{3} \to \frac{10}{3} < x < 10$$

28) The answer is 1.

The intersection of two functions is the point with 2 for x. Then:

$$f(2) = g(2) \quad \text{and} \quad g(2) = (2 \times (2)) - 3 = 4 - 3 = 1$$

Then, $f(2) = 1 \to a(2)^2 + b(2) + c = 1 \to 4a + 2b + c = 1 \quad$ (i)

The value of x in the vertex of the parabola is: $x = -\frac{b}{2a} \to -2 = -\frac{b}{2a} \to b = 4a \qquad$ (ii)

In the point $(-2, 5)$, the value of the $f(x)$ is 5.

$$f(-2) = 5 \to a(-2)^2 + b(-2) + c = 5 \to 4a - 2b + c = 5 \quad \text{(iii)}$$

Using the first two equation:

$$\begin{cases} 4a + 2b + c = 1 \\ 4a - 2b + c = 5 \end{cases} \to$$

Equation 1 minus equation 2 is:

(i)$-$(iii) $\to 4b = -4 \to b = -1 \qquad$ (iv)

Plug in the value of b in the second equation:

$$b = 4a \to a = \frac{b}{4} = -\frac{1}{4}$$

Plug in the values of a and be in the first equation. Then:

$$\to 4\left(\frac{-1}{4}\right) + 2(-1) + c = 1 \to -1 - 2 + c = 1 \to c = 1 + 3 \to c = 4$$

the product of a, b and $c = \left(-\frac{1}{4}\right) \times (-1) \times 4 = 1$

29) The answer is 60.

The relationship among all sides of special right triangle

$30° - 60° - 90°$ is provided in this triangle:

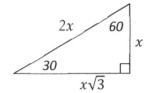

In this triangle, the opposite side of $30°$ angle is half of the hypotenuse.

Draw the shape of this question:

The latter is the hypotenuse. Therefore, the latter is 60 ft.

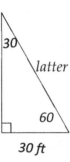

30) The answer is 3.

Let x be the length of an edge of cube, then the volume of a cube is: $\quad V = x^3$

The surface area of cube is: $\quad SA = 6x^2$

The volume of cube A is $\frac{1}{2}$ of its surface area. Then:

$x^3 = \frac{6x^2}{2} \rightarrow x^3 = 3x^2$, divide both side of the equation by x^2. Then:

$$\frac{x^3}{x^2} = \frac{3x^2}{x^2} \rightarrow x = 3$$

31) The answer is 5.

$3x + 6y = \frac{-3y^2 + 15}{x}$, Multiply both sides by x.

$$x \times (3x + 6y) = x \times \left(\frac{-3y^2 + 15}{x}\right) \rightarrow 3x^2 + 6xy = -3y^2 + 15$$

$$\rightarrow 3x^2 + 6xy + 3y^2 = 15 \rightarrow 3 \times (x^2 + 2xy + y^2) = 15 \rightarrow x^2 + 2xy + y^2 = \frac{15}{3}$$

$x^2 + 2xy + y^2 = (x + y)^2$, Then:

$$\rightarrow (x + y)^2 = 5$$

PSAT Mathematics Practice Tests Explanations

PSAT Mathematics Practice Test 2

Section 1 – No Calculator

1) Choice D is correct

$3x - 5 = 8.5 \rightarrow 3x = 8.5 + 5 = 13.5 \rightarrow x = \frac{13.5}{3} = 4.5$

Then; $5x + 3 = 5\,(4.5) + 3 = 22.5 + 3 = 25.5$

2) Choice B is correct

Number of biology book: 35

Total number of books; $35 + 95 + 80 = 210$

the ratio of the number of biology books to the total number of books is: $\frac{35}{210} = \frac{1}{6}$

3) Choice B is correct

$\alpha = 180° - 112° = 68°$

$\beta = 180° - 135° = 45°$

$x + \alpha + \beta = 180° \rightarrow x = 180° - 68° - 45° = 67°$

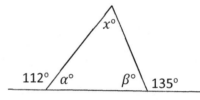

4) Choice D is correct

A. $f(x) = x^2 - 5$ if $x = 1 \rightarrow f(1) = (1)^2 - 5 = 1 - 5 = -4 \neq 5$

B. $f(x) = x^2 - 1$ if $x = 1 \rightarrow f(1) = (1)^2 - 1 = 1 - 1 = 0 \neq 5$

C. $f(x) = \sqrt{x + 2}$ if $x = 1 \rightarrow f(1) = \sqrt{1 + 2} = \sqrt{3} \neq 5$

D. $f(x) = \sqrt{x} + 4$ if $x = 1 \rightarrow f(1) = \sqrt{1} + 4 = 5$

5) Choice D is correct

$xp + 2yq = 26 \rightarrow xp = 26 - 2yq$ (1)

$xp + yq = 17$ (2)

(1) in (2) $\rightarrow 26 - 2yq + yq = 17 \rightarrow 26 - yq = 17 \rightarrow yq = 26 - 17 = 9$

6) Choice D is correct

Let x be all expenses, then $\frac{22}{100}x = \$660 \rightarrow x = \frac{100 \times \$660}{22} = \$3000$

He spent for his rent: $\frac{27}{100} \times \$3000 = \$810$

7) Choice A is correct

$12x^2 + n = a(x^2 + 3)(x^2 - 3) = ax^4 - 9a \rightarrow a = 12$ And $n = -9a = -9 \times 12 = -108$

8) Choice C is correct

$\frac{1}{8} = 0.125 \rightarrow C = 5$

$\frac{1}{20} = 0.05 \rightarrow D = 5 \rightarrow C \times D = 5 \times 5 = 25$

9) Choice C is correct

Let P be circumference of circle A, then; $2\pi r_A = 18\pi \rightarrow r_A = 9$

$r_A = 3r_B \rightarrow r_B = \frac{9}{3} = 3 \rightarrow$ Area of circle B is; $\pi r_B^2 = 9\pi$

10) Choice B is correct

$f(x) = x^2 + 2x - 5$

$f(3t^2) = (3t^2)^2 + 2(3t^2) - 5 = 9t^4 + 6t^2 - 5$

11) Choice C is correct

y is the intersection of the three circles. Therefore, it must be odd (from circle A), negative (from circle B), and multiple of 5 (from circle C).

From the options, only -5 is odd, negative and multiple of 5.

12) Choice C is correct

let x be total number of marbles in the box, then number of red marbles is: $x - 132$

$p = \frac{1}{4} = \frac{x - 132}{x}$

Use cross multiplication to solve for x.

$x = 4(x - 132) \rightarrow x = 4x - 528 \rightarrow 3x = 528 \rightarrow x = 176$

13) Choice C is correct

Plug in the values of x in each equation and check.

I. $(-2)^2 - 2 + 6 = 4 - 2 + 6 = 8 \neq 0$

   $(3)^2 - 3 + 6 = 3 - 3 + 6 = 12 \neq 0$

II. $2(-2)^2 - 2(-2) = 8 + 4 = 12 \rightarrow 12 = 12$

   $2(3)^2 - 2(3) = 18 - 6 = 12 \rightarrow 12 = 12$

III. $5(-2)^2 - 5(-2) - 30 = 20 + 10 - 30 = 0$

   $5(3)^2 - 5(3) - 30 = 45 - 15 - 30 = 0$

Equations II and III are correct.

14) The answer is 66.

In the equilateral triangle if x is length of one side of triangle, then the perimeter of the triangle is $3x$. Then $3x = 33 \rightarrow x = 11$ and radius of the circle is: $x = 11$

Then, the perimeter of the circle is: $2\pi r = 2\pi(11) = 22\pi$

$$\pi = 3 \rightarrow 22\pi = 22 \times 3 = 66$$

15) The answer is 472.

$\dfrac{12}{100}x = 72 \rightarrow x = \dfrac{72 \times 100}{12} = 600$

$\dfrac{1}{8}y = 16 \rightarrow y = 8 \times 16 = 128$

$\rightarrow x - y = 600 - 128 = 472$

16) The answer is 150.

Let b be the amount of time Alec can do the job, then,

$\dfrac{1}{a} + \dfrac{1}{b} = \dfrac{1}{100} \rightarrow \dfrac{1}{300} + \dfrac{1}{b} = \dfrac{1}{100} \rightarrow \dfrac{1}{b} = \dfrac{1}{100} - \dfrac{1}{300} = \dfrac{2}{300} = \dfrac{1}{150}$

Then: $b = 150$ minutes

17) The answer is 1.

$$ax + b = 4$$

When $x = 4$ the value of y equal to zero. (when a line intersects the x-axis, the value of y of the intersection point is zero).

Plug in the value of the x and y of the point (4, 0) in the equation of the line. Then:

$$ax + b = 4 \rightarrow a(4) + b(0) = 4 \rightarrow 4a = 4 \rightarrow a = 1$$

Section 2 – Calculator

1) Choice C is correct

The amount of money for x bookshelf is: $100x$

Then, the total cost of all bookshelves is equal to: $100x + 800$

The total cost, in dollar, per bookshelf is: $\dfrac{Total\ cost}{number\ of\ items} = \dfrac{100x+800}{x}$

2) Choice C is correct

$\sqrt{x} = 4 \rightarrow x = 16$

then; $\sqrt{x} - 7 = \sqrt{16} - 7 = 4 - 7 = -3$ and $\sqrt{x - 7} = \sqrt{16 - 7} = \sqrt{9} = 3$

Then: $\left(\sqrt{x - 7}\right) + \left(\sqrt{x} - 7\right) = 3 + (-3) = 0$

3) Choice B is correct

The angles on a straight line add up to 180 degrees. Then:

$x + 25 + y + 2x + y = 180$

Then, $3x + 2y = 180 - 25 \rightarrow 3(35) + 2y = 155$

$\rightarrow 2y = 155 - 105 = 50 \rightarrow y = 25$

4) Choice B is correct

The distance of A to B on the coordinate plane is: $\sqrt{(x_1 - x_2)^2 + (y_1 - y_2)^2} = \sqrt{(10 - 4)^2 + (11 - 3)^2} = \sqrt{6^2 + 8^2}$

$= \sqrt{36 + 64} = \sqrt{100} = 10$

The diameter of the circle is 10 and the radius of the circle is 5. Then: the circumference of the circle is: $2\pi r = 2\pi(5) = 10\pi$

5) Choice C is correct

Square root of 16 is $\sqrt{16} = 4 < 6$

Square root of 25 is $\sqrt{25} = 5 < 6$

Square root of 37 is $\sqrt{37} = \sqrt{36 + 1} > \sqrt{36} = 6$

Square root of 49 is $\sqrt{49} = 7 > 6$

Since, $\sqrt{37} < \sqrt{49}$, then the answer is C.

6) Choice A is correct

$-3a + 5a + 7a = 45 \rightarrow 9a = 45 \rightarrow a = \dfrac{45}{9} = 5$

Then; $\dfrac{3a-2}{2} = \dfrac{3(5)-2}{2} = \dfrac{15-2}{2} = 6.5$

7) Choice C is correct

All integers from 11 to 19 are: 11, 12, 13, 14, 15, 16, 17, 18, 19

The mean of these integers is: $\dfrac{11+12+13+14+15+16+17+18+1}{9} = \dfrac{135}{9} = 15$

8) Choice A is correct

$|-12 - 5| - |-8 + 2| = |-17| - |-6| = 17 - 6 = 11$

9) Choice D is correct

$g(-2) = g(x = -2) = 3$

$g(3) = g(x = 3) = -2$

$3g(-2) - 2g(3) = 3(3) - 2(-2) = 9 + 4 = 13$

10) Choice B is correct

let x be the number of gallons of water the container holds when it is full.

Then; $\dfrac{7}{24}x = 3.5 \rightarrow x = \dfrac{24 \times 3.5}{7} = 12$

11) Choice C is correct

$(3^a)^b = 81 \rightarrow 3^{ab} = 81$

$81 = 3^4 \rightarrow 3^{ab} = 3^4$

$\rightarrow ab = 4$

12) Choice B is correct

Since, E is the midpoint of AB, then the area of all triangles DAE, DEF, CFE and CBE are equal.

Let x be the area of one of the triangle, Then: $4x = 100 \rightarrow x = 25$

The area of DEC $= 2x = 2(25) = 50$

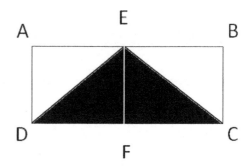

13) Choice A is correct

$13 < -3x - 2 < 22 \rightarrow$ Add 2 to all sides.

$13 + 2 < -3x - 2 + 2 < 22 + 2$

$\rightarrow 15 < -3x < 24 \rightarrow$ Divide all sides by -3. (Remember that when you divide all sides of an inequality by a negative number, the inequality sing will be swapped. < becomes >)

$$\frac{15}{-3} > \frac{-3x}{-3} > \frac{24}{-3}$$

$-8 < x < -5$

14) Choice A is correct

First find the number of pants sold in each month.

January: 110, February: 88, March: 90, April: 70, May: 85, June: 65

Check each option provided.

    A. January and February,

$$\left(\frac{110 - 88}{110}\right) \times 100 = \frac{22}{110} \times 100 = 20\%$$

    B. February and March, there is an increase from February to March.

    C. March and April

$$\left(\frac{90 - 70}{90}\right) \times 100 = \frac{20}{90} \times 100 = 22.22\%$$

    D. April and May: there is an increase from April to May

15) Choice D is correct

First, order the number of shirts sold each month:

$$130, 140, 145, 150, 160, 170$$

median is: $\frac{145+150}{2} = 147.5$

Put the number of shoes sold per month in order:

$$20, 25, 25, 35, 35, 40$$

mean is: $\frac{20+25+25+35+35+40}{6} = \frac{180}{6} = 30$

16) Choice D is correct

Let x be the number of shoes needed to be added in April.

$$\frac{70}{20+x} = \left(\frac{5}{17}\right)\left(\frac{85}{25}\right) \rightarrow \frac{70}{20+x} = \frac{425}{425} = 1 \rightarrow 70 = 20 + x \rightarrow x = 50$$

17) Choice C is correct

The value of y in the x-intercept of a line is zero. Then:

$$y = 0 \rightarrow 2x - 2(0) = 5 \rightarrow 2x = 5 \rightarrow x = \frac{5}{2}$$

then, x-intercept of the line is $\frac{5}{2}$

18) Choice A is correct

The sum of the lengths of any two sides of triangle is greater than the length of the third side, therefore the greatest possible value of the biggest side equal to 4 cm. $4 < 6$

19) Choice A is correct

The quadrilateral is a trapezoid. Use the formula of the area of trapezoids.

$$Area = \frac{1}{2}h(b_1 + b_2)$$

You can find the height of the trapezoid by finding the difference of the values of y for the points A and D. (or points B and C)

$$h = 8 - 2 = 6$$

AB= $\sqrt{(x_1 - x_2)^2 + (y_1 - y_2)^2} = \sqrt{(6-3)^2 + (8-8)^2} = \sqrt{9+0} = 3$

CD= $\sqrt{(x_1 - x_2)^2 + (y_1 - y_2)^2} = \sqrt{(8-2)^2 + (2-2)^2} = \sqrt{36+0} = 6$

Area of the trapezoid is: $\frac{1}{2}h(b_1 + b_2) = \frac{1}{2}(6)(3+6) = 27$

20) Choice D is correct

Choose a random number for a and check the options. Let a be equal to 15 which is divisible by 5, then:

A. $a - 1 = 15 - 1 = 14$ is not divisible by 4
B. $a + 1 = 15 + 1 = 16$ is divisible by 4
   but if $a = 5 \rightarrow a + 1 = 5 + 1 = 6$ is not divisible by 4
C. $2a = 2 \times 15 = 30$ is not divisible by 4
D. $2a - 2 = (2 \times 15) - 2 = 28$ is divisible by 4

21) Choice B is correct

$(x - 2)^3 = 27 \rightarrow$ Find the third root of both sides. Then:

$$x - 2 = 3 \rightarrow x = 5$$

$$\rightarrow (x - 4)(x - 3) = (5 - 4)(5 - 3) = (1)(2) = 2$$

22) Choice B is correct
Number of Mathematics book: $\qquad 0.3 \times 840 = 252$
Number of English book: $\qquad 0.15 \times 840 = 126$
Product of number of Mathematics and number of English book: $\quad 252 \times 126 = 31752$

23) Choice D is correct
The angle α is: $0.3 \times 360 = 108°$
The angle β is: $0.15 \times 360 = 54°$

24) Choice C is correct

According to the chart, 50% of the books are in the Mathematics and Chemistry sections.

Therefore, there are 420 books in these two sections.

$0.50 \times 840 = 420$

$\gamma + \alpha = 420$, and $\gamma = \frac{2}{5}\alpha$

Replace γ by $\frac{2}{5}\alpha$ in the first equation.

$$\gamma + \alpha = 420 \to \frac{2}{5}\alpha + \alpha = 420 \to \frac{7}{5}\alpha = 420 \to multiply\ both\ sides\ by\ \frac{5}{7}$$

$$\left(\frac{5}{7}\right)\frac{7}{5}\alpha = 420 \times \left(\frac{5}{7}\right) \to \alpha = \frac{420 \times 5}{7} = 300$$

$$\alpha = 300 \to \gamma = \frac{2}{5}\alpha \to \gamma = \frac{2}{5} \times 300 = 120$$

There are 120 books in the Chemistry section.

25) Choice A is correct

Let x be the number of years. Therefore, $2,000 per year equals $2000x$.

Starting from $24,000 annual salary means you should add that amount to $2000x$.

Income more than that is:

$I > 2000\ x\ +\ 24000$

26) Choice C is correct

The area of the trapezoid is:

$$Area = \frac{1}{2}h(b_1 + b_2) = \frac{1}{2}(x)(13 + 8) = 126$$

$$\to 10.5x = 126 \to x = 12$$

$$y = \sqrt{5^2 + 12^2} = \sqrt{25 + 144} = \sqrt{169} = 13$$

The perimeter of the trapezoid is: $12 + 13 + 8 + 13 = 46$

27) Choice A is correct

$$|x - 2| \geq 3$$

Then:
$x - 2 \geq 3 \to x \geq 3 + 2 \to x \geq 5$
Or
$x - 2 \leq -3 \to x \leq -3 + 2 \to x \leq -1$
Then, the solution is: $x \geq 5\ \cup\ x \leq -1$

28) The answer is $4\sqrt{3}$.

Based on triangle similarity theorem: $\frac{a}{a+b} = \frac{c}{3} \rightarrow c = \frac{3a}{a+b} = \frac{3\sqrt{3}}{3\sqrt{3}} = 1 \rightarrow$ area of the shaded region is: $\left(\frac{c+3}{2}\right)(b) = 4\sqrt{3}$

29) The answer is $\frac{\sqrt{8}}{3}$.

$\sin(A) = \frac{opposite}{hypotenuse} = \frac{1}{3} \Rightarrow$ We have the following triangle, then:

$c = \sqrt{3^2 - 1^2} = \sqrt{9 - 1} = \sqrt{8}$

$\cos(A) = \frac{\sqrt{8}}{3}$

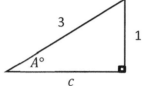

30) The answer is 80.

One liter=1000 cm$^3 \rightarrow$ 6 liters = 6000 cm^3

$6000 = 15 \times 5 \times h \rightarrow h = \frac{6000}{75} = 80$ cm

31) The answer is 12.

$\begin{cases} 2x = x + 3y - 5 \\ 4x = 2y - 10 \end{cases} \rightarrow \begin{cases} x - 3y = -5 \\ 4x - 2y = 10 \end{cases}$ Multiply first equation by (-4), then

$\begin{cases} -4x + 12y = 20 \\ 4x - 2y = 10 \end{cases}$ Add two equations:

$\rightarrow 10y = 30 \rightarrow y = 3 \rightarrow x = 4 \rightarrow x \times y = 12$

"Effortless Math Education" Publications

Effortless Math authors' team strives to prepare and publish the best quality PSAT Mathematics learning resources to make learning Math easier for all. We hope that our publications help you learn Math in an effective way and prepare for the PSAT test.

We all in Effortless Math wish you good luck and successful studies!

Effortless Math Authors

Online Math Lessons

Enjoy interactive Math lessons online

with the best Math teachers

Online Math learning that's effective, affordable, flexible, and fun

Learn Math wherever you want; when you want

Ultimate flexibility. You can now learn Math online, enjoy high quality engaging lessons no matter where in the world you are. It's affordable too.

Learn Math with one-on-one classes

We provide one-on-one Math tutoring online. We believe that one-to-one tutoring is the most effective way to learn Math.

Qualified Math tutors

Working with the best Math tutors in the world is the key to success! Our tutors give you the support and motivation you need to succeed with a personal touch.

Online Math Lessons

It's easy! Here's how it works.

1- Request a FREE introductory session.

2- Meet a Math tutor online.

3- Start Learning Math in Minutes.

Send Email to: info@EffortlessMath.com

Made in the USA
Middletown, DE
21 March 2019